WINFIELD'S WALNUT VALLEY FESTIVAL

SETH BATE

INCLUDES REFLECTIONS BY WORLD-RENOWNED MUSICIANS
DAN CRARY, BEPPE GAMBETTA AND JOHN McCUTCHEON
AND BLUEGRASS RADIO PERSONALITY ORIN FRIESEN

Published by The History Press
Charleston, SC
www.historypress.com

All images are courtesy of the Walnut Valley Association unless otherwise noted.

First published 2022

Manufactured in the United States

ISBN 9781467146050

Library of Congress Control Number: 2022936618

CONTENTS

FOREWORD

By Kendra Redford

While this book is likely to be published in 2022, just in time for our fiftieth Walnut Valley Festival (WVF), I am writing this in November 2020. Yes, 2020, the year that serves as a watershed in our personal and national history, separating what came before from what came after. Even as I write this, we aren't quite through this pandemic, but there is reason to hope that 2021 will be a better year.

This book contains both researched history and recollections of individuals. I have a few memories to share and, for better or worse, they are intertwined with expressions of my gratitude.

Primarily, I would like to thank Seth Bate. Many of you know Seth from his stints as an emcee during the festival, although his connection extends back further. Seth's wife, Jennifer, is the daughter of Joe Muret, one of the original founders of the festival. Seth and Jennifer serve as the hosts for our Wednesday workshops. Seth produced the definitive history of WVF as his thesis for his history degree at Wichita State University. When I first read it, I remember telling my son, Bart, "He nailed it!" Seth was able to combine a genuine love for his subject matter with firsthand knowledge gleaned from years of experience. Couple that with the scholarly mind required to organize and utilize extensive research on the subject, and you have a winner. He conducted interviews with many who were involved in those early years of the festival, including his father-in-law and me, and it shows. The thesis is

The main entrance with a part of the Avenue of Flags, 2018.

available online (soar.wichita.edu/bitstream/handle/10057/15473/t18005_Bate.pdf?isAllowed=y&sequence=1 or https://bit.ly/3sH44cN).

Seth's work is intended to be the core of this book. Since the book is also a celebration of fifty years' worth of sweat equity, we wanted to include the perspectives of those who have made it possible for the festival to still be going strong. Because of the dedication and sharp eyes of our photography crews over the years, we had thousands of photographs to pick from. It was a great gift to have so many options, and it was a tough job to choose.

We reached out to performers, emcees, office staff, gate workers—a range of people we hope are representative—to tell us what it is that makes Winfield special for them. Those who have come over the years will know many of the writers, but we wanted you to hear from those who work behind the scenes as well. You'll hear the stories of some campers, as well as a few who organize campground stages each year. I want to thank each and every person who contributed to this book to help us celebrate a very special milestone.

Fifty years! It hardly seems possible. Bob and I were in still in our thirties when he was approached by Joe Muret and Stuart Mossman about producing a music festival. Back then, Bob was an insurance salesman and the festival was just a side project, but it gradually grew to become his primary job. It was always his passion. From the very first festival, he was continually thinking about it and trying to improve it. Over the years, there have been so many people who have contributed their time, energy and a heck of a lot of hard work to help make this festival into what it is today—a permanent resident of a very special place in all our hearts. I think back on all those great people we came to know because of their involvement in our festival, and I am grateful.

Some folks came from afar to arrive at Winfield and work on setup for the festival (or help tear down). But many were locals who took a "vacation" every year to put in long hours on the grounds to make every festival memorable. People in Winfield are proud of the fact that we can be in an airport in Denver, Cincinnati or maybe even Rome and spot a shirt that says "Winfield." We are proud of the fact that our city's name has become synonymous with contests that bring the most talented musicians from all over the world to compete for a title that people understand makes them the best of the best.

Several couples worked for us, many times pairing up to run a specific area. Troy and Michelle Boucher ran crafts for many years. More recently,

Kendra and Bob Redford in the audience, 1989.

Paulette Rush ran the arts and crafts fair with the help of her husband, Alan. When Paulette passed away in 2018, we renamed the arts and crafts fair in her honor. Art and Leota Coats worked on press and communications for us. Paul and Zoe Doolittle ran the ticket trailer with good humor for so many years. Louise Logsdon organized our contests, and her husband, Johnny, was one of our best-loved emcees. Ed and Jeannine Foster inherited and ran the contests after the Logsdons retired. It was, of course, a family affair. My sister, Frances, for a long time, oversaw reentry. I also stepped in and helped Bob run things once the festival became so big that it was nearly impossible for one person to manage. All four of our kids were involved as they grew up—they didn't have a choice, really. I am proud to say that my son Bart and my daughter Krys, as well as my grandson Kevin, work the festival to this day.

We were one big extended family, and I think that was felt on the midway and in the campgrounds. There were so many music festivals that were started in the 1970s that didn't survive the 1980s or 1990s. I am proud that ours is still going strong. I think that is due, in large part, to the fact that so many of our patrons feel like they are coming home to Winfield every year. And for my family—the Walnut Valley family—we always felt like the third weekend in September was a huge family reunion.

And the entertainers! So many became part of our Walnut Valley family and would tell us that they always looked forward to their annual pilgrimage to Winfield. They told us that we treated them like real people, and we did, for better or worse. Our chuckwagon, run by the capable crew overseen by Becky and John Conway, has been a magical place where performers have sat down alongside staff and crew and been served hearty meals capped by award-winning desserts. Entertainers who have played at Winfield tell tales of this strange and fantastical place called the "Grove" and of how much fun they had just wandering around and joining in jams or playing on one of the campground stages after a late-night set on Stage I.

We have lost some of these entertainers—quite a few, honestly—who played at Winfield in the early years: Doc Watson, John Hartford, Tut Taylor, Bill Barwick and Cathy Barton. I'm sure many others belong on the list. But a new generation has literally grown up on the grounds, surrounded by mentors and supporters: Nickel Creek, Erin Mae, Scenic Roots, the members of Driven, Pretend Friend and Old Sound. We are so grateful that Andy May took a chance on establishing his Acoustic Kids here. We are excited by the possibilities of our Feisty Music Camp and are also grateful for the work of the talented organizers of this venture, Erin Mae, Peter Lague and Aaron

Above: The Paulette Rush Arts and Crafts Show is named for WVA secretary Paulette Rush. From 1988 to 2017, Paulette and her husband, Alan, coordinated the show. In 2018, Alan presented the first "Paulette Prize" to crafter Pete Knapp (*center*) and his associate in the Music Kitchen.

Right: Since its early days, festival operations have been divided among crews, each with a crew chief. The festival experience depends on the crews that handle responsibilities, such as parking, security and groundskeeping. Krys Redford, shown here in 2010, is a crew chief for the grounds.

Korra Mongkhonvilay (*left*) and Caroline Blas (*right*) try out a mountain dulcimer during Feisty Music Camp for Kids in 2018. The music camp is part of a long Walnut Valley tradition of inviting young people to try out acoustic string instruments.

Fowler (as well as so many others who stop by to sing, dance and play over the weekend), who help little ones enjoy their time at Winfield.

And the fans—well, so many people have written about the unique experience at the Winfield Fairgrounds, and that is mostly due to the hospitality of the campers who show up year after year (and earlier and earlier each year, it seems) with their unique camp names and traditions. As far as I am concerned, it is now as much their festival as it is ours. And I know that many of them feel the same way. This is a pickers' festival, where you can count on seeing scores of people of every age gathered around a campfire or under an awning, or even just walking down one of the many lanes in the campgrounds, jamming until the wee hours of the morning and beyond. If you are one of these people, I hope you will see some part of the festival you know and the love reflected in these pages.

Several years ago, when we asked people to recount their favorite memories of Winfield, many chose 2001 as the year they remembered most clearly. The stages opened just two days after the terrible tragedy of September 11, and people felt shell-shocked; they debated over whether to come. Our little town of Winfield, so far away from that terrible attack, served as a sanctuary

Pickers and players pose in an attempt to create the world's largest string band in 1991. The Walnut Valley Festival also twice tried to set a world record for the world's largest guitar band. Rex Flottman had heard of a guitar festival in Germany attempting to achieve a *Guinness Book of World Records* listing for hosting the largest guitar band. He shared the story with Bob Redford. At first, Redford suggested they go over there and see it happen. "But his eyes really got big [when Flottman said], 'We're in 'Pickers Paradise.' We should have the record here.'...Bob liked the idea, and it was off and running."

for those who gathered to grieve and maybe—just a bit—to heal. John McCutcheon drove day and night to get here (barely) in time to perform. Other groups and performers were trapped, unable to fly in, and local and regional performers agreed to come to help fill the gaps in our schedule. And the performances where people joined hands to sing songs like "This Land Is Your Land," led by our singers and songwriters—well, I think those are the memories that have been burned into people's minds. Those are some of the memories that make my Winfield, your Winfield, special.

If you are reading this, you probably have Winfield memories of your own. I hope this book brings them to mind. Maybe it will inspire you to write a few of them down or post a photograph online. You might phone an old campmate or put on an album you haven't played in a long time.

The Walnut Valley Men's Chorus, directed by Keith Anglemyer, and the Walnut River String Band perform together on Stage I in 2002.

Mostly, though, I hope this book gets you excited to come back next year to see what has changed, enjoy what is familiar and make some new memories. And if you are reading this because you're curious about our festival but have never made the trip, you are especially invited. As someone once said about Winfield, every year is the best year to come.

ACKNOWLEDGEMENTS

There is extraordinary goodwill surrounding the Walnut Valley Festival, and it has been evident in the enthusiasm so many folks have shown for this project.

First, thanks to my thesis advisor, Dr. Jay Price, who pointed out that as key anniversaries loom, institutions are often ready to have their stories told. Thanks to Keith Wondra, whose presentations about his own publishing process made this book seem possible. Thanks to Bob Hamrick for blessing this history as a complement to his gorgeous *September's Song*. And it's impossible to write about this music without tipping a hat to bluegrass scholar Neil V. Rosenberg.

Thanks of course to all the contributors who generously shared what the Winfield experience has looked like through their eyes. A particular thanks is owed to Orin Friesen, who wrote a beautiful chapter and also offered thoughtful comments on the manuscript and pushed to get the facts correct.

The Walnut Valley Association staff has put up with my questions and intrusions for years now. Thanks especially to Bart Redford for believing and investing in this effort and to Rex Flottman, Kevin Redford and Karen Deal for finding, fixing and filling in images and information.

My own sharp-eyed mom, Jan Gugeler, offered expert proofreading, and my ukulele buddy and editor Shannon Littlejohn gave the whole thing a final buffing.

Thanks to my in-laws, Joe and Christie Muret, for their memories of the early years. To my family—Seaf, Emma and Jenny—I love you, and I plan on having another fifty years of camping and singing together.

To the other emcees and stage managers, I take great pride in being part of our crew. Hugs and high fives to all of you.

Finally, if you are reading this and have ever been part of this festival, thank you for what you have added to the community. I hope we'll run into each other in the campground. I'm usually hiding behind my talented friend Terry, applauding the hot pickers and waiting for a three-chord folk song to break out. Say hi, and let's find a song we both know.

Seth Bate

1

SOUTHWESTERN FOLK AND WINFIELD BLUEGRASS

By Sam Ontjes

Sam Ontjes is a banjo player and former employee of the S.L. Mossman Company. With cooperation from his friends and the support of administrators at Southwestern College in Winfield, Kansas, Ontjes put together a folk festival that borrowed elements of the Newport Folk Festival. Some of those elements would also become familiar parts of the Walnut Valley Festival.

The first Southwestern College Folk Festival in the spring of 1968 came at a time of youthful idealism, exploration and uncertainty. A lot of us knew we were headed for Vietnam as soon as we graduated.

Our sympathies with the peace and civil rights movements coincided with our interest in folk music. The folk festival grew out of a deep love several students had for acoustic roots music, their desire to share that love and the willingness of administrators to indulge them and try something different.

Looking back, it amazes me that Dr. Douglas Moore, the dean of students, and the Cultural Arts Council gave us $2,000 and turned us loose. Our budget was limited, but thankfully, we didn't have to concern ourselves with making a profit.

I acted as the director, and Stuart Mossman did publicity. Many students—too numerous to name—helped with everything from publicity and selling tickets to creating the printed program, soliciting sponsorships, setting up, running the stage and sound and finding housing for performers. We were having so much fun, our grades probably suffered, but most instructors were sympathetic. It was an exciting time.

The Winfield community was known for supporting all things involving Southwestern College, and the folk festival was no different. The program listed thirty-five businesses and individuals who signed on as patrons.

Our objective was to introduce students and the community to folk music beyond the popular commercial groups like the Kingston Trio. We wanted to include a variety of styles ranging from blues to bluegrass and hoped people would appreciate the diversity. I think they did. Doc Watson's warmth and amazing guitar won over the audience, regardless of whether they liked his music. Vern and Ray and Herb Pedersen drove to Winfield from Nashville and played their hearts out for one hundred dollars. They played not only in a scheduled performance but also in a chapel service and other venues on campus. After hearing them, uninitiated skeptics realized that bluegrass music involved admirable sincerity, instrumental prowess and spine-chilling harmonies. After performing the blues on stage Friday night, living legend and ex-sharecropper Mance Lipscomb continued performing at the Black Eye, the college coffee house, until the early hours of Saturday morning. We don't know when he finally quit.

Jimmy Driftwood's down-home story songs appealed to people of all ages. Written as a history lesson, his familiar "Battle of New Orleans" resonated. Pat and Victoria Garvey introduced original songs about the Old West. Art Eskridge sang railroad songs and cowboy songs that were passed down from his family. Charlie Cloud, a folklore professor from Kansas State University, told stories.

Aside from concerts on Friday and Saturday nights, the Southwestern Festival included a Sunday morning gospel sing, workshops, demonstrations, open mic and jamming sessions and camping, all emulating the Newport Folk Festival. Subsequent Walnut Valley Festivals incorporated these features, as did many other folk and bluegrass festivals that cropped up around the country.

A second folk festival took place at Southwestern College in 1971, featuring Dan Crary and David Bromberg, but I had graduated by that time and was not involved. It was called both the Southwestern College Folk Festival and the Walnut Valley Folk Festival.

Despite the similarities between the Southwestern College Folk Festival and the later Walnut Valley Association Festival, they differed in some notable ways. The scale of the WVA festival was greater, and it was intended

Jimmy Driftwood commands the stage. Driftwood, who wrote such standards as "Tennessee Stud" and "The Battle of New Orleans," was on the bill at the Newport Folk Festival and created the Arkansas Folk Festival. Driftwood played for the Southwestern College Folk Festival, three Walnut Valley Festivals and the Spring Thing. Driftwood and his wife, Cleda, grew close to WVA organizers, especially Art and Leota Coats.

to turn a profit. A larger venue at the fairground and more capital enabled the WVA to sign contracts with more performers. With bigger names, organizers anticipated a larger crowd.

The WVA Festival focused on bluegrass rather than the broad definition of folk that the Southwestern College festivals followed. The bill ran the bluegrass style gamut from traditional with Lester Flatt, Jim and Jesse, the Lewis Family, the Stone Mountain Boys and the Bluegrass Country Boys to progressive with New Grass Revival and Byron Berline and the Country Gazette.

From left to right: Norman Blake, Dan Crary and Doc Watson trade tunes in 1980. The curated all-star jams staged at the WVF seemed to amplify both the camaraderie and the competitiveness of the performers, making for compelling listening and lasting memories.

Plans for that first WVA festival included contests for guitar flat-picking and bluegrass bands. Regional bluegrass associations in Kansas, Arkansas, Missouri, Oklahoma, Texas, Nebraska and Colorado responded. Denver, Oklahoma City and Dallas held promise as potential audience sources beyond the immediate area of Wichita, Lawrence, Manhattan and Kansas City.

Some of the people involved in the Southwestern Folk Festival also worked on the first WVA Festival in 1972. There was broad interest in starting a festival, but the event only became a reality when Bob and Kendra Redford stepped up with the money. In addition, the Southwestern College Cultural Arts Council contributed, allowing students to attend for free.

Stuart Mossman, Joe Muret and the rest of us who were working at Mossman Guitars enthusiastically pitched in to help. No one was paid. Our excitement grew from a love of the music, the chance to meet musicians we admired and the potential for promoting our guitars. I fondly remember the

Local women demonstrate lye soapmaking at an early Walnut Valley Festival, whose organizers relied on local expertise for the educational aspects of the festival. Interactive demonstrations and hands-on activities, particularly those for children, have remained a part of the festival.

months of anticipation before the festival, when we would listen all day to recordings of the Country Gazette, Dan Crary, Doc Watson and New Grass Revival while sanding and finishing guitars in the shop.

In addition to taking tickets and setting up the grounds, we gave tours of the guitar shop and worked the Mossman booth under the grandstand. That provided a great opportunity to meet performers and fans, to demonstrate guitars and jam. For years, Mossman Guitars staff helped, doing grounds work, taking tickets, acting as emcees and judging contests. But the most important part for many of us was jamming in the campgrounds and under the grandstand.

Pickers Paradise became a reality. For me, it was even more fun than the Southwestern College festival because I didn't have to worry so much about logistics and got to play. It was heaven.

Unfortunately, the attendance at the first WVA Festival suffered from terrible weather. Freezing temperatures and rain put a damper on things. Those of us who attended still had a great time, but it wasn't enough to cover the expenses. Despite the initial setback, Bob and Kendra Redford deserve a lot of credit for hanging in there and continuing in subsequent years. To them and their family, we all owe a big vote of thanks for their perseverance and an incredible fifty years.

2

ATTENDING IN THE EARLY YEARS

By Wayne Steadham

The culture and traditions of the festival have been shaped by fiercely dedicated fans. In addition to supporting the festival in various ways, Wayne and Diane Steadham were among the very first of the fans who endured all kinds of weather to hear—and play—music. These fans camp as close to the same spot as they can each year.

Is it good luck, karma or being in the right spot at the right time? The people I describe here all consider themselves to be on the right side of karma for the experience known as Walnut Valley Festival.

The first festival held at the Cowley County Fairground in 1972 was largely experimental and an effort to appeal to the growing number of acoustic guitar music enthusiasts. Organizers chose elite players who were available for appearances on the stage and established a contest to determine the best flat-picking guitar player in the land. The draw for me was to impress my then-girlfriend, Diane Riggs, with music and hear a new hero, Norman Blake. Also on the bill were Doc Watson with his son Merle and T. Michael Coleman. Lester Flatt appeared with his band, and Jim and Jesse were there with the Virginia Boys. We sat in the grandstand and listened to every act. For the finale, the flat-pickers Norman Blake and Dan Crary joined legend Doc Watson for a fiddle tune show that still lingers in authenticity and pure enjoyment for me.

Wayne Steadham (*left*) and Debbie Biddle (*right*) work in the site office in 1989. The trailer was the hub of communication for staff and a check-in spot for most workers, who were scheduled nearly around the clock. This office was one of the first pieces to move in during setup and one of the last to go when things were taken down and moved to storage. It was also the location for staff members to grab a bottle of water and a snack while they shared the day's best stories and cooked up new ideas.

Diane's mother, Frances Riggs, was a veteran of the fairground grandstands, so she sent an old wool army blanket with us. She said if we didn't need it for comfort from the cold, at least we could sit on it.

Along with these all-star pickers were Country Gazette, New Grass Revival and Bluegrass Country. All of these acts were in their dawning years, but individual members would stand out in later years. For Diane and me, the best part of the new event was when the emcee asked, "If you had a good time, would you come back next year?" "Great idea," we thought, "only change the date to the third weekend in September, and maybe it won't snow." It did indeed snow during the three-guitar jam late at night. The woolen army blanket was handy for sure.

Diane and I have gone back every year and have always been inspired by the people and music. From the first event to the latest one, the evolution

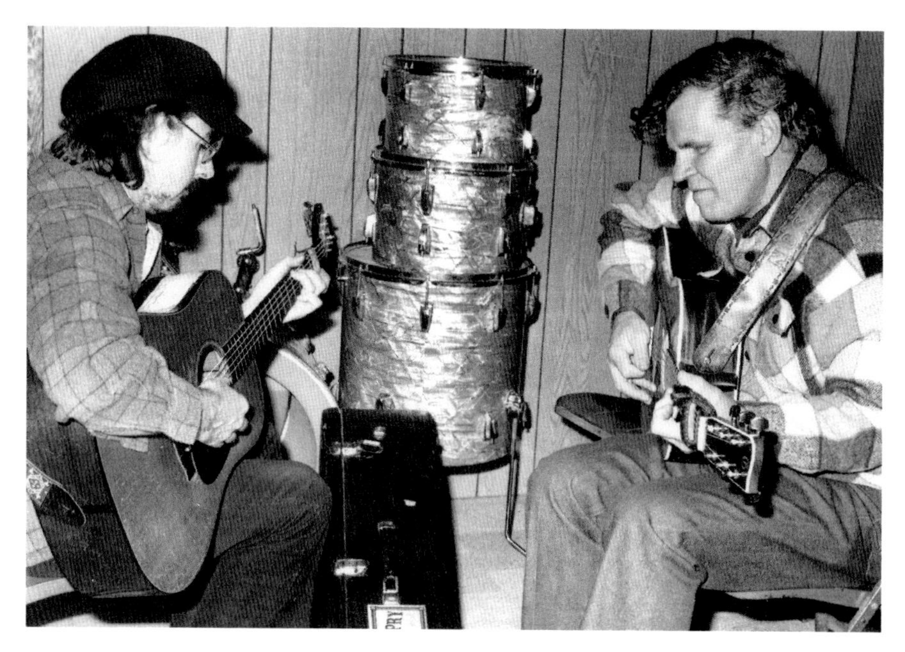

Norman Blake (*left*) and Doc Watson (*right*) jam backstage in 1974.

of the festival has been continual. Diane (friends call her Diney) and I are always excited for the September ritual, and we relish in the inventive people who are attracted to Winfield.

The second WVF found Diney ready, woolen army blanket in hand. We sat near the sound board for every show. The music had instilled a passion in us. Our introduction to the world of acoustic music was an important step in our lives, and we have become much better people for it. From the stage, John Cohen of the New Lost City Ramblers told of musicians playing in the campground. His take was that this is a wonderful thing because sharing music is the best.

Like others, I took my guitar and camped in the Pecan Grove, looking for like-minded players. My abode was an army surplus pup tent. I played John Prine songs and Bob Dylan songs but realized the fiddle tunes were being played by a group of older men in the west campground. Joe Sanders, the Winfield fire chief, was a lover of fiddle tunes. He borrowed a funeral canopy from the funeral home and erected it for the weekend in the west campground. This was the picking area for fiddlers, guitar players and folks wanting to listen to "authentic" picking instead of a stage show.

Ben Green, Pete Davis and John Logsdon, along with Joe Sanders, led the local picking contingent. Cotton Combs, Big Joe and others in the jam session were from Arkansas, Missouri and Oklahoma. The sharing of musical information came easily, and a picking etiquette was born and observed. Lunchtime came at the jam session on Saturday, and all the players wanted something to eat that would not break up the music. The closest camper produced fresh tomato sandwiches on white bread, and they multiplied and were shared as if it were a religious gathering.

Bob and Vernita Westbrook moved from Boulder to open a music store in Winfield, which was quickly growing into its "Pickers Paradise" moniker. Their store, the Pickin' Post, was the local provider of everything a player needs. Bob was a master craftsman, specializing in banjo building and instrument repair. He and Vernita played locally as a duo and became prized Winfield citizens. They opened the store in the evenings so jam sessions could have a home. Like his craftwork, Bob's playing was precise, and his influence on the jam session was monumental. Our friendship with Bob and Vernita led to introductions to Jimmie and Shirley Booe and Kenny and Jo Glasgow.

Soon, our excitement for the music led us beyond Winfield. We all met up at the Haysville Bluegrass Festival, where Orin Friesen was the host and emcee. Orin was also a performer and emcee at the Winfield festival, and we all listened to his bluegrass radio show on KFDI. Another festival in nearby Bentonville, Arkansas, was the next step in our exploration—a great place for the Westbrooks, the Booes, the Steadhams and the Glasgows to meet and even see Royce Campbell of Langley, Oklahoma. Royce's band, Natural Grass, featured flat-picking and great songs. Westbrook had done repair work on Royce's guitar.

Diney and I upgraded to a blue canvas tent for the Bentonville festival. Soon, Jimmie, Shirley, Kenny and Jo arrived in their camping units. The Booes were sporting a just-modified Dodge van, and the Glasgows had an overhead camper on their pickup truck. Bob and Vernita camped in their truck and had a canopy for picking shelter. This camp arrangement in the Bentonville Fairgrounds led to a discussion on how we could improve our arrangements the next time we camped at Winfield. The spot Jimmie and Kenny favored on the west side of the pole barn was heavily shaded, and we agreed it would be our shared site in the future.

At Bentonville, all of us took on the responsibility of spreading the word about the Winfield festival. We spoke of the legendary jam sessions to an often very skeptical bluegrass audience. These early years of successive jaunts to bluegrass festivals both far and near meant seeing familiar faces at nearly every venue.

Opposite, top: Kenny Glasgow and his bass, pictured here in 1990, anchor a daytime jam. One of the first campsites to have a name and a consistent location was the Pickin' Parlor.

Opposite, bottom: Members of Bluestem, *(from left to right)* Jim Rood, Marvin Pine and Stan Rood, pose in front of their likenesses at Stage IV in 1992. The painting by Dayton and Sandra Wodrich of Brenham, Texas, was one of a series of portraits of memorable festival characters.

Above: In 1974, after coming through the festival entrance, each car turned east to park or turned west to camp.

Kenny and Jo Glasgow refurbished an abandoned building on their property in Rainbow Bend. Kenny invited pickers to enjoy their hospitality in the Picking Parlor. Many players loved the weekend jam sessions that were taking place regularly.

Norman and Vicky Selberg came to Winfield to paint signs for the festival. Norman asked us to call him Rat. Vicky said it was because he was such a rat. His talents as a painter and picker were readily accepted by all of us. Rat came to our usual campsite at the festival, the site of many shared meals and jam sessions, and brought a sign that designated our camp the Pickin' Parlor Branch Office. The name reflected Rat's point that the prime gathering spot for musicians was the Glasgows' Pickin' Parlor, but during the festival, the prime spot was at the fairgrounds under the pole sheds.

Bonnie Carol (mountain dulcimer) joins in some campground picking beneath the power plant. The power plant on the hill is one of the landmarks that help orient people on the festival grounds. South of the power plant is the Pecan Grove. North of the plant is the West Campground.

Others will tell the stories of who, when and what the temperature was. The story of the Pickin' Parlor Branch Office is about the people who have become friends. This friendship goes beyond most normal definitions, and we can be most easily defined as a family. We gather annually, share meals and accolades and commiserate in our grief. We celebrate achievements and always welcome new members.

3

"WE WANTED TO DO SOMETHING FOR WINFIELD"

By Seth Bate

The folk festivals at Southwestern College in 1968 and 1971 demonstrated that people in and around Winfield, Kansas, had some appetite for acoustic music, especially when performed by elite guitar players. An ambitious luthier and the people who worked for him were traveling to folk and bluegrass festivals to spread the word about the guitars they were building, and they naturally thought that bringing music lovers from other locales closer to their factory would be both fun and good for business. Meanwhile, a civic-minded Winfield businessman who was burned out on hosting motorcycle rallies was open to new projects that would help his community and, if possible, turn a profit. A farmer who was friends with them both helped forge a connection, and the Walnut Valley Festival debuted in 1972.

The Walnut Valley Association was founded in the living room of a small farmhouse with a native stone fireplace a few miles south of Winfield, Kansas, in March 1972. Joseph and Christie Muret, a couple in their twenties, were hosting Bob Redford and his wife, Kendra, who farmed east of Winfield and operated an insurance office in Winfield. Bob and Joe were loyal members of the Winfield chapter of Jaycees, more formally the United States Junior Chamber of Commerce, a service club that capped the age for members at forty. The two men had collaborated on a number of Jaycees projects over the years, including an annual motorcycle rally at the Winfield Fairgrounds.

The back cover of the 1972 souvenir program. The first festival was sponsored by the newly formed WVA, along with the Southwestern College Cultural Arts Series.

Muret, a farmer and cabinetmaker, had been working at the S.L. Mossman Guitar Company part time in exchange for a guitar. In his frequent conversations with Redford, Muret would share news about the guitar shop and its founder, Stuart Mossman. Mossman was often on the road, traveling to music festivals, and he brought back glowing stories of the music he had heard and the people he had met. He kept pestering Muret to join in the trips so he would not miss the fun. Muret preferred to stay home, mind the quiet shop and stay current with his farm chores.

"Finally," Muret said, "I told him kind of to get him off my back about going to Mountain View....If they had a music festival in Winfield, I would go to it....That sort of not-serious comment led to him saying, 'Well, if I had $10,000, I could put on a music festival in Winfield.' That led me into

The schedule for the first WVF featured traditional bluegrass, with acts such as Lester Flatt and the Nashville Grass; new grass represented by New Grass Revival; and an onstage guitar jam by flat-picking legends Doc Watson, Dan Crary and Normal Blake. It also included an open house at the S.L. Mossman guitar factory a few miles away.

thinking, because of my involvement in Jaycees, young businessman that I was, I could find $10,000."

Muret started talking to Redford about the idea of a Winfield-based festival. "It wasn't an immediate thing. Every time I was with him, I would kind of tell him what a great thing [the guitar shop was] doing....When I went to him with the idea of getting ten people to put money in, his reaction was, 'If it's such a good thing, why get ten people? If you can sell it to me, I'll finance it for us.'"

Both men liked the idea of creating an opportunity that would benefit Winfield businesses and organizations rather than the typical community event that required visiting merchants for sponsorships and donations. They were done with the motorcycle races, which had developed a reputation for rowdiness that some in Winfield did not appreciate.

Knowing that they were on the brink of something that would represent significant work, the Murets and the Redfords sat down at the Muret home to decide if they were fully committed to the idea. The result was the formation of the Walnut Valley Association (WVA) on March 29, 1972, and, in September 1972, the debut of its signature event, the Walnut Valley Festival (WVF) at the Winfield Fairgrounds.

Two folk festivals that had taken place at Southwestern College had provided evidence of a community appetite for such events. Leota Coats, who wrote for the WVA's publications and was married to festival publicity coordinator Art Coats, said the festivals in 1968 and 1971 inspired the WVF. In her memory, community members, including Art Coats, Mossman and Redford, started talking after the first performances at the college about an expanded concert with other associated activities at the fairground, where there was more space. They said, "This should continue. Could we have a festival or something like that?"

The WVA formed around three specific individuals: Mossman, Muret and Redford. Kendra Redford recalled, "Stuart was one of the original founders, Bob was one of the original founders, but Joe Muret was also one of the original founders. He was working in the guitar factory at the time, and in fact, I kind of attribute the original idea or suggestion to him....He said, 'Why don't we have a festival, you know, here in Winfield?' In fact, he's the one that approached Bob for the financing because they had worked in Jaycees together." Muret called himself an intermediary between the luthier and the investor: "Basically, Stuart had a concept, and I took that idea to Bob to finance it."

From left to right: Stuart Mossman, Joe Muret and Bob Redford show the prize instruments for the first National Flat-Picking Contest in 1972. The three were partners in the Walnut Valley Association. Mossman brought his experience of visiting other bluegrass festivals and his network of industry contacts to the association. Muret built the first festival stage and oversaw operations. Redford made the largest initial investment and brought his business acumen to the organization.

Bob Redford represented—and provided—capital, business acumen and administration. Joe Muret handled the operations and the grounds, literally putting blood and sweat into welding the first stage together. Stuart Mossman was the initial force behind booking and maintaining relationships with musical artists; although others quickly filled in, including festival publicist Art Coats and, later, WVA secretary Louise Logsdon, media coordinator Rex Flottman and the Redfords themselves.

The operational areas always bled into one another; indeed, an asset and a vulnerability of the festival's operation was Bob Redford's hands-on approach to all aspects of the festival's production. Still, all three aspects (networks, business acumen and operations) were present from the festival's first year, augmented by the dedication of dozens—and later, hundreds—of other people.

In part because of terrible weather, the first two festivals lost money. Redford told a Kansas Farm Bureau reporter that organizers viewed the situation through an agricultural lens. "I knew Sunday morning that we were going to finish the weekend way down in the red. I was ready to throw in the proverbial towel. But Joe is the typical farmer with a strong constitution, and he convinced me that we were in so far over our heads that the only way out was to hold another festival."

It was with the third festival that everything jelled. The weather was beautiful, and attendance rose 96 percent from the previous year. After "experimenting with various ideas and ways of doing things for two years, things went well. When it was over, we felt like we were beginning to understand how to make a festival operate," Muret said after the event. The first three festivals also set a pattern that would repeat over the years; poor weather would reduce revenue, and the WVA would carry a loss for a year or two to make up for it. "It used to take about a couple of years to come back from what we call the 'lost year,'" Kendra Redford said.

Internally, the WVA made its first shift. Though Mossman continued to make suggestions for acts to hire, he was no longer part of the association. He "had connections or knew the artists because of his guitar factory. [He put] together the first two or three years of the lineup for the festival. But his guitar factory was growing, so it was kind of hard for him to do both," Kendra Redford remembered. The three founders also had some communication issues and some disagreements over who could speak for and make commitments on behalf of the organization.

When Bob Redford bought out Mossman's share, Muret asked for the same treatment out of loyalty to Mossman. Unlike Mossman, however, Muret remained part of the crew for about twelve years. The Redford family owned the corporation—and the risks and rewards that went with it.

To festivalgoers, there was still a strong association between WVA and Mossman Guitars. In 1976, Mossman invited people who were winding down their festival weekend to come by the factory for a Sunday morning tour. In 1977, Mossman Guitar Company advertised in the *Flatlands Occasional*, an attempt by the WVA and Coats to spin the organization's newsletter into a separate publication.

Aside from the core directors—then Redford, Muret and Art Coats—the festival built and refined its network of workers in its first years. Working for a combination of admission to the festival, an hourly wage, a chance to be close to the music and a love of community, these workers developed procedures and traditions as they went. "We did it by involving a lot of people, a lot of volunteers who were our friends, family friends, work friends, associates that had ideas and were tickled to death to work in exchange for a ticket in the beginning," said Muret. "There was really a spirit of 'we want to do something for Winfield.'"

Beginning around 1975, Art Coats (*right*) joined Bob Redford and the WVA as a publicist. Coats supplied articles for publications like *National Bluegrass News* and *Pickin'* and wrote official publications. He also befriended many of the festival's entertainers. Art's wife, Leota, also became a staff writer.

The WVA explored ways to branch out, including investigating a partnership in Japan. Organizers even tried to launch a couple more festivals of their own. In 1976, organizers staged a second festival, the Spring Thing. Christie Muret, who helped run and schedule workers for the ticket trailers, said that event was the exception to the good behavior she came to expect from the festival crowd. "People just came to have a good time. They weren't looking for trouble. All except the Spring Thing. That was a different deal." The Spring Thing did not return the next year. Kendra Redford recalled, "We thought, 'OK, we won't do a second festival.' We had a pretty good crowd, but we decided it was too much work.

"Well, we kind of forgot that piece of advice, and we tried again in 1979."

The forgetful planners dubbed their next attempt at a second festival the June Jamboree. Kendra Redford said the lineup of acts was wonderful; it included Magpie, Ed Snodderly, Joel Mabus, Art Thieme, Cathy Fink and Duck Donald, Gamble Rogers, and Jay Ungar and Lyn Hardy. (A few years later, Ungar would write "Ashokan Farewell," an enduring modern fiddle tune.) The crowds were thin, however. "We lost money on the June Jamboree, but we made enough money in the fall that we didn't have that big of a loss," Kendra Redford said. That time, the decision to hold only one festival a year stuck—mostly.

The WVA experimented with promoting a two-day concert event at the Starlight, an amphitheater in Kansas City, Missouri, on August 1 and 2, 1987. Performers included the Seldom Scene, Mike Cross, and Jack and Mike Theobald and Bluegrass Country. Orin Friesen remembered the days as two of the hottest of the year.

Ultimately, focusing on a single event was an important part of sustaining the WVA. Workloads increased, and the operation required months of planning each year. Kendra Redford said, "People would ask us, you know, 'Are you working on the festival now?' And they didn't realize we were working on the festival year-round."

4
THE GREAT TWENTIETH-CENTURY GUITAR RUSH

By Dan Crary

Dan Crary of Placerville, California, is a flat-picking guitar pioneer and a scholar of the steel-string guitar. He has been a member of several influential bands, including California and Berline, Crary and Hickman. Crary played at Southwestern College in 1971, and he is the only artist to appear on the bill of the first twenty Walnut Valley Festivals. He also shaped the format and style of the National Flat-Pick Guitar Championship.

In the 1840s in California, it was the gold rush. Fifty years ago in Winfield, Kansas, it was the guitar rush.

Fifty years—it's hard to imagine. In the early '70s, your grandpa who came to Winfield was a young guy who had long hair and played the guitar badly. The Age of Aquarius was raging, the war dragged on, Luckys tasted better and your house had a black-and-white TV with rabbit ears. The radio played the hits of Roberta Flack, Neil Diamond and Don McLean. (Remember "American Pie?" No, of course not. You weren't born yet.) Watergate was just an office building somewhere, and coming soon were Tony Orlando and Dawn, Jimmy Carter, the Captain and Tennille and a whole bunch of other fun stuff—so much, it's painful to remember.

Fifty years seems like a very long time. But you must realize, the Walnut Valley Festival (popularly known as Winfield) brings the best acoustic music of America here every year and has for all of those fifty years. For a lot of people out here in middle America, way off center from the folk music

Flat-pickers Pat Flynn (*left*) and Kenny Smith (*right*) enjoy an anecdote from Dan Crary (*center*) on Stage II in 2011.

revival of the '50s or the first bluegrass festivals of the '60s, Winfield was their first direct contact with the American acoustic music movement. It brought them all those things that go along with acoustic music: families with kids, campgrounds with jam sessions and shared food and a community for a weekend, as strangers and their families became friends and neighbors for a few days, with guitar music at the center. And of course, they experienced the definitive professional acoustic musicians of the time right here, a few feet away, up on that festival stage.

Historians of the 1840s gold rush emphasize how gold fever brought Americans together to meet each other from all over the country for the first time. In the 1970s in Winfield, it was the guitar rush: Americans from all over the country traveled here with their families and steel-string guitars; camped out in tents, sleeping bags and campers; bought tickets to hear music in a grandstand; and jammed through the night with people from all over whom they had never met before.

And they still do; while the gold rush fizzled out after a few years, the Winfield guitar rush continues unchecked, raging into the future. Winfield's golden anniversary seems like a good time to celebrate and reflect on what is happening here.

BUILT AROUND THE STEEL-STRING GUITAR

When it all started, I was trying to be a musician and a graduate student (aiming to become a professor) all at once. So, I was never around the office enough to be a definitive historian of the organization behind the festival. The first guys who cooked up the original idea for the festival I ever talked to were Stuart Mossman, a luthier and founder of Mossman Guitars, and Bob Redford, a Winfield businessman. I know now that there was a third member of the triad, Joe Muret, who had brought Bob and Stuart together. Their vision and conversations about the festival were pretty advanced when they invited me to perform for the first festival in 1972, and they had me help plan and judge the festival guitar contest.

But one thing was clear about the vision they had: They wanted to build it around the steel-string guitar. Other instruments, including banjos,

Left: Steve Kaufman picks a tune after winning the National Flat-Picking Championship for the third time in 1986. Kaufman won three "contest-consecutive" years in a row. He first took the title in 1978. Contest rules required winners to sit out for five years; when Kaufman was again eligible in 1984, he won again. In 1986, the contest was open to all, and Kaufman won again. A prolific producer of instructional books and videos, Kaufman presides over a popular series of camps for musicians.

Right: Molly Tuttle picks a solo on Stage I in 2018. Tuttle was the first woman named the International Bluegrass Music Association Guitar Player of the Year. In addition to the flat-picking and crosspicking approaches to guitar, Tuttle created her own innovative clawhammer guitar style.

A roomful of flat-pickers try out what they have learned from instructor Dan Crary in the parlor at First Baptist Church in Winfield. During the festival, there are workshop sets placed on the stages. These usually consist of several instrumental specialists demonstrating a style or technique and answering audience questions. On the Wednesday before the festival, some entertainers offer additional hands-on workshops at the church.

mandolins, fiddles, dobros and autoharps, were to be included, but the guitar was front and center. It was my honor and joy to say yes.

It's hard to realize today, but building a festival around the steel-string guitar was a pretty out-there, forward-thinking idea in the early '70s. The old flattop acoustic steel-string guitar had been a sort of background member of various types of acoustic music—always there but in a support role. When I started to play in 1952, the word "flat-picking" was country slang, and the number of flat-pickers on the radio was one (Hank Snow). Then in the later '50s, the folkies favored strumming the nylon-string guitar.

In the '50s and '60s bluegrass, the guitar was almost always just a rhythm instrument, almost never playing a lead role or calling attention to itself. Nationally, Doc Watson was a field of one. In country music and rock, the electric guitar was dominant. It's even difficult to explain why the steel-string guitar is an almost totally different instrument from these other versions of guitars. Its full name, the "flattop steel-string acoustic guitar" is a jaw-

Steve Mason works on an instrument in 2011. Mason is a familiar face under the grandstands each year at the Steve Mason Luthiers and Violin booth. He was a guitar maker with the S.L. Mossman Company in the 1970s and a member of the Lawrence, Kansas–based Alferd Packer Memorial String Band. Mason's popular blog is called *Ask a Luthier*.

breaking nine syllables long; you have to enroll in a two-hour workshop to even learn how to talk about the thing.

That means in 1971, it was way out there and far-sighted for Bob, Stuart, Joe and their guitar-loving friends to think that this instrument was to be the centerpiece of a popular event that, fifty years later, is the premier showcase for great acoustic music, especially steel-string guitar music. You have to give it to those old guys—they called it right.

Because they had this foresight, we now celebrate Winfield by doing exactly what the founders envisioned, picking, singing, camping, sharing food and meeting other people who all love guitar music and listen for the voice of God behind the strings. You and I are lucky; we are the generation that has been most accompanied by guitar music, the generation of the great guitar rush.

They don't call the guitar an "instrument" for nothing; it has been instrumental in getting neighbors and strangers together, bringing beauty and peace into a tough world and cutting across lines that divide us. The steel-string guitar is our great gift, and the Walnut Valley Festival, celebrating fifty years, is its home.

5

AND THE WINNER IS

The Walnut Valley Association Contests

By Jeannine and Edward Foster, with updates from Karen Deal

The original version of this article was part of the 2007 Celebrate Winfield History event. Ed and Jeannine Foster served as coordinators of the Walnut Valley Association instrumental contests from 1993 to 2008. They succeeded Johnny and Louise Logsdon, who ran the contests for the first twenty years. From 2009 to today, Karen Deal has been the contest coordinator. While some of the personnel have changed and processes have been refined since the original article was written, anyone who observed a contest in the Foster era and again in 2019 would find the experiences very similar.

Winfield has a rich tradition in music dating back to its earliest years. While much of its music has been of the religious, classical and band varieties, the name Winfield has more recently become identified with folk and bluegrass music. In 1972, the WVA organized for the purpose of producing the Walnut Valley National Flat-Pick Championship contest. The flat-pick contest served as the anchor for the contests that followed; it also promoted proficiency in playing the guitar. Later contests inspired excellence with other acoustic instruments.

In 2006, the festival observed its thirty-fifth anniversary. It was an exciting festival for many reasons, including the return of several winners to defend their titles from previous years. Jimmy Gyles, the flat-pick winner from 1972 and 1973 and the mandolin winner from 1974, presented the prizes to the flat-pick winner, Matthew Arcara. Gyles was a professional musician and

Contest official Johnny Logsdon congratulates Jimmy Gyles on winning the first Walnut Valley Mandolin Championship in 1976. The contest's top three participants were all finalists in other events that year. Gyles also took third place in the National Flat Pick Guitar Championship. The mandolin runner-up in 1976 was Orrin Star (*left*), who won the flat-picking contest. Third place went to Mark O'Connor (*right*), who was also crowned the Walnut Valley Old Time Fiddle Champion.

a member of Mountain Smoke, a group that performed at the festival six times over the years.

In the history of the contests, there are dozens of winners who have had notable careers, but three are legends.

The prodigy Mark O'Connor made his mark in the early contests. Not only did he win the fiddle contest and finish second in the flat-pick competition at the age of thirteen, but O'Connor also came back the following year and won the guitar contest. In 1976, O'Connor nabbed another second-place finish with the fiddle, and in 1977, he became a two-time National Flat-Pick Champion. O'Connor would go on to have a stellar career as a solo and session musician and had high-profile collaborations with Yo-Yo Ma and Edgar Meyer. He has won three Grammy Awards. O'Connor returned for the first time as a festival performer in 1983 and returned seven more times.

Mark O'Connor, age fourteen, plays in the 1975 Walnut Valley Old Time Fiddle Contest, backed up by his ten-year-old sister, Michelle O'Connor, on fiddle and Greg Morton on guitar. O'Connor was the fiddle champion in 1974 and 1977, and he was the National Flat-Pick Guitar Champion in 1975 and 1977. O'Connor has released nearly fifty albums since 1974, appeared on countless recordings by other artists and received three Grammy Awards.

Alison Krauss sings in 1991, the year after winning her first Grammy Award. One of her first public musical successes was winning the Walnut Valley Old Time Fiddle Contest in 1984. Krauss was also a third-place finisher in 1986. Krauss ultimately won more Grammys than any other female artist—a total of twenty-seven.

Twelve-year-old Chris Thile holds his prize Davis mandolin after winning the National Mandolin Contest in 1993. Reporter Susan Rife wrote that Chris's youthful exuberance could not be contained when he and two other finalists were called backstage to learn the judges' decision. "Holy cow! I won!" Chris yelped. The crowd erupted into laughter and applause. Thile told Rife he wanted to be a professional baseball player rather than a full-time musician. As it turned out, Thile went on to have a stellar musical career, which included five Winfield appearances with his band, Nickel Creek.

Alison Krauss won the Walnut Valley Old Time Fiddle contest in 1984 at the age of thirteen. Krauss followed her Winfield win with a string of championships around the country. Krauss came back to Winfield as a performer in 1988, 1991 and 1993. She won her first of an astonishing twenty-seven Grammy Awards in 1990.

Chris Thile won the mandolin contest in 1993 at the age of twelve. "Holy cow! I won!" yelled Thile backstage, ruining the surprise onstage reveal but earning laughter and applause from the audience. The next year, the prodigy returned as a stage performer with his band, Nickel Creek. Thile has since won four Grammy Awards and a MacArthur Foundation "Genius" Fellowship.

THE LOGSDON YEARS

The first National Flat-Pick Guitar Contest in September 1972 was won by fourteen-year-old Jimmy Gyles from Tahlequah, Oklahoma. That same year, Country Mile from Norman, Oklahoma, won the Walnut Valley Bluegrass Band Championship.

Beginning with the second festival, new contests were added: Walnut Valley Old Time Fiddle (1973), National Bluegrass Banjo (1974), National Mountain Dulcimer (1976), Walnut Valley Mandolin (1976), Tut Taylor National Dobro (one year only, 1976), National Hammer Dulcimer (1977), National Finger Style (1979), International Autoharp (1981), International Finger Style (2004, replacing National Finger-Pick) and National Mandolin (2010, replacing Walnut Valley Mandolin). The Bluegrass Band Championship was discontinued after five years. There was some inconsistency in the way contests were referenced; for instance, "finger-pick," "finger pick," "finger style," and "fingerstyle" all showed up in print at various times to describe the same contest.

Lynn Morris collects the first-place trophy for the National Bluegrass Banjo Contest in 1974. Morris came back to win the contest again in 1981, and she is still the only female champion. Morris appeared at Winfield as a performer in the band Whetstone Run in 1979 and 1983 and then with the Lynn Morris Band in 1991. In her career, Morris earned three Female Vocalist of the Year Awards from the International Bluegrass Music Association.

Ron Penix of Baltimore, Maryland, is delighted to win the third-place trophy in the inaugural International Autoharp Championship in 1981. Penix played autoharp starting as a child and was a friend of Mother Maybelle Carter, who helped popularize the instrument. Martin Schuman of Gainesville, Florida, won the first autoharp contest. Bonnie Phipps of Denver, Colorado, took second place and returned to win in 1982 and again in 2014.

All these contests evolved under the leadership of Louise and Johnny Logsdon. After Johnny became a contest emcee, Louise devised a plan to improve the registration process. In 1974, she began to direct all the contests. Working at first in her home, she organized all the contestants' names into the separate contests. In 1977, as a full-time employee at the office, she devised a simplified system, in which each of the contests would have a separate file folder. She also developed a manual for ordering supplies, provided instructions for the judges and auditors and assembled a contest registration book, known as the contest "Bible."

Some contest regulations were borrowed from the Kansas Oldtime Fiddlers, Pickers and Singers, an organization to which Louise and Johnny belonged. Under their direction, the festival initiated a rule that first-place winners must wait five years before competing again in the same contest.

The Logsdons were later joined by their daughter Judy Irvin, who helped backstage; Judy's husband, Ron, who was in charge of the auditors and judges; and Linda and Grady Boulier, their other daughter and son-in-law who assisted with various festival contests.

Early on, the fiddle and mandolin contests were held in the horse barn, now the mercantile locale, where judges and auditors were situated in a secret and obscure corner. The flat-pick and banjo contests were held on the grandstand stage. The two dulcimer contests were held on Stage III, behind the Winfield Community Theater barn. All contests were later moved inside to Stage IV, where the sound could be controlled and wind and cold weather could not interfere.

Ron Irvin recalled that one year during the banjo contest, a tornado warning sounded as two contestants were waiting to play. When asked about continuing the contest, the audience shouted back, "Go on and finish!" When the last musician finished playing, everyone trooped to the shelter and waited for the storm to pass.

It was the Logsdon family's duty to carry all the prize instruments from the contest booth to the grandstand stage to present them to the winners. One year, it rained so much that the track in front of the stage dissolved into a muddy quagmire. As Louise slogged through the mud, she lost her lovely white shoes. She continued on barefoot with the instruments, laughing all the way across the track to the stage.

A guitar player makes his way to Stage I over the mud on an improvised walkway of pallets. Festival organizers and attendees have devised many creative ways to stay out of the mud, using wood chips, plastic sheeting and hay bales. Newcomers asking for advice online are often told to pack their swimming suits, rain boots and parkas in order to make it through the weekend comfortably.

Johnny, himself a talented musician, could quickly tell when a contestant was about to be disqualified because of some rule infraction. One rule forbade using a slide on a guitar because of the kind of sound it produced. For many years, without fail, Johnny would tell Catfish Keith, a guitar player, "Now, Keith, you're a good player. You deserve a chance to win this contest. So, keep that slide in your pocket. You know that the judges will disqualify you." Keith would listen, get settled, smile and then look squarely at Johnny and proceed to play—using the slide. But because he was such a good player and a good showman, the crowd would go wild. After his performance, he would zip over to the barn and sell an amazing number of his tapes. He continued to do the same for many years, disqualifying himself every time by using the forbidden slide.

As the number of contestants began to increase, it became necessary to add more staff. In 1988, Dennis Moran and Edward Foster joined the announcing staff.

THE FOSTER YEARS

When the Logsdons retired in 1992, Edward and Jeannine Foster were appointed as the new contest coordinators, and the staff was expanded to include Dennis Moran and Julie Davis as emcees and Shirley Booe as office coordinator. Lou Ann Schmidt, Kristy Koebele and Carolyn Voss later served on the contest staff and helped update and expand the contest system as it moved from paper files to computers. Karen Deal later joined the crew as an assistant to the Fosters. Other festival workers filled in as needed.

In the summer of 1987, Rex Flottman, a photographer who had recently moved to Winfield, stopped by the office for information about the festival. After visiting with Bob Redford, he was offered a job to take some pictures during the next festival. He was to take portraits of the three winners in each of the eight contests, along with candid photographs of the grounds. The next year, he was responsible for all the photographs with the help of Milie Winchester. Others who helped with the photography and publicity included Larry Junker, the editor of a daily newssheet that was distributed on the grounds during the festival; Ned Graham, who contributed stories for the newssheet; and photographers Debbie McNinch, Gary Hanna and Dan and Pam Cribbs. Their pictures were valuable to the winners and the donating luthiers for publicity purposes.

Other workers who had significant responsibilities included Paulette and Alan Rush, who also spent years in charge of crafts and the information booth. Beginning as a part-time secretary, Paulette was later promoted to executive secretary. Her duties included, among many others, processing contest entries and ordering plaques, trophies and belt buckles for the winners. During the festivals, the Rushes took charge of displaying and transporting the prize instruments and trophies.

The judges, all of whom remain anonymous, are a very important part of the contest process. They are chosen from past winners and performers and vary from year to year. There are five judges for each of the two guitar contests and three for each of the other six contests. Housed in a separate building, they neither see the contestants nor hear the backup players. Contestants are not allowed to speak on the mic, which means judges hear only the instrument they are evaluating. Judges fill out evaluations for each musician and do not discuss them among themselves.

Because the judges are sequestered, they sometimes have a different experience than the audience. Dennis Moran recalled one fiddle contest when one of the musicians was an attractive young woman wearing a fetching western outfit. This, along with her stage presence and good performance, endeared her to the audience. When the judges awarded her only a second-place award, the crowd showed its disappointment and anger by booing loud and long. Later, a judge explained, "Sorry, but we just pay attention to how they play. Besides, we couldn't see her."

The results are tabulated by the two auditors under the direction of the head auditor, who, for many years, was Dean Bradbury, a Winfield CPA. After his death in 2005, he was replaced by Anne Richardson and Carolyn Verbeck. The judges do not provide contestants with suggestions for improvements; their job is only to choose the top three winners.

Judges who want to change the rules are told, "This is the way the rules are written, and Bob Redford expects us to follow them." One of these rules prohibits the use of certain songs, such as "Orange Blossom Special" and "Black Mountain Rag." In the early years of the contests, several judges insisted on this rule if they were to continue judging because those tunes were played so frequently—and often poorly.

In addition to their pay, the judges are given a gift. In the past, this had been a Gott ice chest or drink container. Now, they receive a mug that is handmade by the Elk Falls Pottery Company; on each mug, "Here come da judge" is printed. The mugs have become so popular that many judges hope to eventually accumulate a set of them.

Contest Legends and Lore

Memorable things occasionally occur because the musicians are nervous and under pressure or because of the conditions on the stage. Some are funny; others are not. One year, shortly after a tall and husky man began to play, his chair collapsed with a resounding crash, and he slid to the floor, clutching his precious guitar. A horrified gasp arose from the audience. After backstage workers rushed to his aid, he got up, checked his guitar and, with a new chair, began again. His nerves of steel were rewarded: he took second place.

Louise remembered a twenty-six-year-old redheaded man who came with several buddies to register. As he signed up for the flat-pick contest, his friends suggested that he also sign up for the mandolin and fiddle contests. When he admitted that he had neither the money nor the instruments, they offered to lend him both. He signed up for all three and won first place with both the mandolin and the fiddle. He did not place with the guitar. Karen Deal said she did not know about this specific incident, but similar scenarios are familiar. "I can't tell you how many times [a contest staff member has] slipped the entry fee to a contestant with empty pockets," she said. "We've all purchased day tickets for contestants at some point, too."

While the stories of young and energetic contestants are memorable, contest staff have also seen their share of competitors who are older, in poor health or both. In some cases, contestants with terminal conditions have entered one more time as a bucket list item. Karen Deal remembered two men who competed at times when just getting on and off the stage required significant effort and bravery—Dave Peters, when he won the Walnut Valley Mandolin Championship in 1995, and Kelly Lancaster, when he won the same contest in 1998.

Both men lived in Nashville, occasionally collaborated with each other and were well known for their studio work as fiddle and mandolin players. Peters played on the first Dixie Chicks album. Lancaster recorded with Alison Krauss. Deal said each man entered that contest thinking it could be his last. For both of them, Deal recalled, "Their friends helped them to the stage, and their friends practically carried them off the stage after their performance. The performance between those two acts of love were beyond memorable; they were heavenly. Just to watch and hear them play raised the hair on my arms and rendered me breathless." Peters died in 1999. Lancaster died in 2013.

Not everyone who registers actually gets on the stage to play. Occasionally, a musician will register and pay the fee but back out and forfeit the ten dollars (later fifteen) after seeing the quality of the competition.

One Winfield native is also a contest title holder. Karen Mueller, then nineteen, was the first contestant on the stage at the first International Autoharp Championship in 1981. She did not win, but she said she learned a lot that year: "[A]lthough I was technically competing against other players, the challenge was more personal. I had to think carefully about my song selections, arrange them by developing interesting variations and learn them well enough to play them in my sleep. I also learned that much of it was out of my hands, like the luck of the draw, and I shouldn't stop trying." Mueller finished in third place in 1985, and she won the championship in 1986.

Following the Contest Book

The steps and procedures for administering the contests changed very little over the first thirty-five years of festival activity. Originally, all contestants registered only by mail or by signing up on the grounds prior to the contest. Later, registrations were accepted by mail, email, telephone, fax or in-person during the contests. As technology advanced, so did the options for registration. The only qualifications for registration are signing up, paying the registration fee and having the courage to play on a stage before a large audience.

As interest grew, it became necessary to limit the number of players to forty per contest in order to not overwhelm the judges. Many years, the guitar contests filled up long before festival week. The standby process was developed as an answer to this problem.

One afternoon as Jeannine was working the registration table, a man came dashing up to enroll, explaining that he had taken the day off from work and had been driving nonstop across several states to play in the fingerstyle contest. When he was told the contest was already closed, tears came to his eyes. Looking over the registration list, Jeannine noticed several spots were reserved for regional contest winners. Some of them had not yet checked in and, judging from previous years, she guessed not all of them would come. Jeannine told the fingerpicker that if he would register, pay his ten-dollar fee and show up ready to play, there was a good chance there would be a place for him. If not, he would get a refund. With a big grin, he signed up and paid the fee. Fortunately for him, several registrants did not appear, and he was allowed to compete.

The luthiers who produce the award instruments are an important part of both the contests and the festival itself. Many of them have booths under the grandstand, where they sell instruments, along with cases, strings and other supplies. Of those instruments given as awards, many are donated by these luthiers. Their values vary according to the instrument, the wood from which they are crafted and additional decorative features, such as mother-of-pearl inlays. The values of these instruments and the cash awarded each festival have dramatically increased over the years. In 1972, with two contests, the total value was $4,325; by 2005, with eight contests, it had risen to $89,735. The total prize package for 2021 was $113,462. As of 2021, with the help of participating luthiers, the WVA has awarded more than $2.6 million in cash, instruments, trophies and prizes.

One luthier who has been committed year after year is hammer dulcimer builder and player Russell Cook. Cook first attended in 1979, and he won the National Hammer Dulcimer Contest in 1981. Every year since, he has appeared at the festival as a performer, contestant and/or sponsor of the contest. Most years, the dulcimer built by Cook's company, Master Works, has been the instrument selected by the first-place winner.

All of the prize instruments available to festival contestants are displayed, 1980. According to Rex Flottman of the festival staff, this image is exceptionally rare. Bob Redford requested a photograph like this every year. Because of last-minute deliveries and competing pressures, however, the photograph rarely happened.

Shadows stand out against the Stage III backdrop during a late afternoon set in 2015. Autoharp champion Jo Ann Smith was on stage with Patricia Webster (bass), Scott Schmidt (mandolin) and Jesse Smith (guitar, not pictured).

Sometimes, a prize instrument launches a winner into another level of achievement. JoAnn Smith said that happened to her after winning the autoharp contest in 1999. "The prize autoharp that year was a wonderful instrument made by Tom Fladmark, a single-key beauty set up in the key of G. To this day, I'm convinced that having that particular instrument placed in my hands at that particular time is what directed my playing from that day forward. Hearing the sweet sound of that autoharp took my playing in a whole new direction."

As often as possible, the luthiers present the prize instruments as the winners are announced. One of these luthiers is Sam Ray Compton, who, for a number of years, presented not only the winning fiddle but also the case and bow. On one occasion, because of the backlog of work at his shop, he was only able to present the back and front of the instrument. To the dumbfounded winner, he explained, "This will give you an idea of how it will look. I'll mail it to you when we put it together." Another time, because the finish was still sticky, he showed the winner a different fiddle, promising he would mail the winning instrument at a later date.

After one flat-pick contest, Jeannine was visiting with the first-place winner, who had previously placed second or third five years in a row. After bemoaning how long it took to finally win first place, he was asked whether he still owned all five guitars. He replied that being recently married, he had sold two in order to rent their apartment. After thinking about it a bit, he admitted, "If I had taken first place the first time, I wouldn't have had all those free instruments."

Other contestants said they would never part with any instrument they had won at the festival. One who had competed over a number of years related his experience as a result of a forest fire in Colorado. After receiving word that his house was in the path of the fire, he set out for home at top speed. When he met his wife on the way, she explained that when she was told to take whatever she could in two minutes time, she grabbed some photo albums and his guitars and ran. He answered, "You did just right!"

We've all heard the expression "the thrill of winning and the agony of defeat." Some people do not fare well under "the agony of defeat." For example, if a contestant wins second place, they may assume that if they practice diligently all year, they will be rewarded the following year with a first-place honor. What they do not take into consideration is that there probably will be different judges next time and many new contestants will be competing. One of them could be a virtuoso.

One year, a young man of seventeen came with his family from western Kansas. He played well and was awarded a second-place trophy and fiddle. The following year, he returned with a large vocal contingent of family and friends, all expecting that he would take first place. He did place among the top five but failed to make the second cut for the final three winners.

After the contest ended and the awards had been made, a commotion of people crowded the backstage area. The young man's grandfather, a very large and formidable individual, furiously bore down on Jeannine, demanding to know why his grandson had not won first place. After all, he had won second place the previous year. They had brought all their friends and relatives along to help celebrate, and it was embarrassing to the family patriarch, who had made such a fuss. The grandmother and the young man cornered Ed and were loudly complaining about the results. Ed and Jeannine did what they could to soothe the family's ruffled feathers, and they finally left, still mumbling angrily.

The next year, as preparations were being made for the fiddle contest, several burly security men broke through the backstage door, demanding, "Where are they?" Somewhat bewildered, the workers asked, "Who are you looking for?" They answered, "We heard the family from western Kansas is back, and we are here to protect you." However, the disappointed lad and his family never appeared again.

Many caring people help run the festival, as illustrated by the following story. A man with limited English language skills arrived at the festival gate in 1990 without enough money to buy a ticket. He had traveled for two days on a Greyhound bus from San Francisco. Having already paid his contest entry fee, he had not understood that he also needed a ticket to enter the grounds. Security workers took him to the site office because they didn't know what to do with him. After one of the workers heard his story, she gave him enough money to buy the required entry ticket. Security then took him back to the entry gate for his ticket and wristband. He played so well that he won third place in the mandolin contest and received a cash reward for it. He then came back to the office and paid back the money with thanks. Two years later, he won first place, and the year after that, he was hired as one of the festival entertainers. His name was Radim Zenkl.

CONTEST PROTOCOL

Winning a contest greatly enhances the careers of those who compete. As a result, entries come in from nearly every state and many foreign countries starting each January.

Some of the contestants come through accredited qualifying contests; at their peak, there were twenty-six of these contests in the United States, Japan, Canada and Australia. In order to qualify, these contests must follow WVA rules and procedures. First-place winners in any of these contests are guaranteed one of forty contestant spots and are given free admission to the festival and the contests.

Because the contests are international, contest staff often found themselves doubling as travel agents and hospitality coordinators. For example, Carolyn Voss assisted a musician from the Philippines to find transportation and hotel accommodations. He and his mother were very grateful.

For a better understanding of contest protocol, it is helpful to follow a contestant through the process from registration to the point of the contest's completion.

Registration closes one hour before the contest begins; all contestants gather in the tent west of the Stage IV barn thirty minutes later. The emcee reads the rules, lists the prizes, takes questions and reads the contestants' names in the order they were registered. Names are drawn to determine the performance order. Each contestant's name is printed on a large white card.

A contestant with a high number may volunteer to play on the stage prior to the actual competition in order to set up the microphone, which is hooked up to the judges' room. Once it is approved by the judges, this mic will not be changed so that all contestants have the same coverage. Competitors are allowed to take the stage with a backup instrumentalist playing rhythm. The sound from the backup's mic is heard only by the audience. The emcee also has a mic, which is heard by both the judges and the audience. For the benefit of those in the audience, the emcee reads the rules and lists the prizes.

When the actual competition begins, the emcee announces, "Judges, this is contestant number one." After the contestant comes on stage, followed by his or her backup, a worker places the white card with the contestant's name and number on a holder. Each musician plays two songs for the first round (three for the fiddle contest). The second contestant follows and so on through the entire list.

Once all the contestants have played, the judges' sheets are tabulated by the auditors. The list of the top five contestants is sent backstage and then announced over the mic by number only so that judges do not hear the contestants' names. After the musicians who made the final cut are all assembled backstage, they again draw numbers for the order of performance. Each contestant plays two more numbers. The judges then select the first-, second- and third-place winners.

After these numbers are announced over the mic, the winners move to the photography room backstage, where the first-place winner chooses from among the prize instruments. The second-place winner chooses from the remaining two and the third-place winner receives the last instrument.

The presentation procedures begin with the emcee awarding a plaque to the two finalists who did not place in the final three. The third-place winner then comes on stage to receive the prize instrument and trophy. At this time, winners may speak on the microphone and play one song. They may also have friends join them. The second-place winner follows. Last of all, the first-place winner receives their chosen instrument, a trophy and other prizes and then plays a final number for the audience.

Following these presentations, members of the media crew interview the winners for publicity purposes and take their photographs. Larry Junker, Melinda Redford, Gary Hanna and Debbie McNinch are among the

Above: *From left to right*: Geoff Bartley, Bill Mize and Stephen Bennett hold their trophies from the National Finger Style Championship in 1985. Bartley was a top-three finisher from 1984 to 1987. Mize won in 1985, after finishing third the year before. Bennett had a third-place finish in the National Flat-Picking Championship in 1983, and he won that contest in 1987.

Right: Muriel Anderson receives her championship Larrivée guitar in 1989 from company representative Cory Thompson. Anderson was the only woman to win the National Finger Style Guitar Championship. The contest was replaced with the International Finger Style Championship in 2004. It has seen two female champions: Helen Avakian (2014) and Christie Lenée (2017).

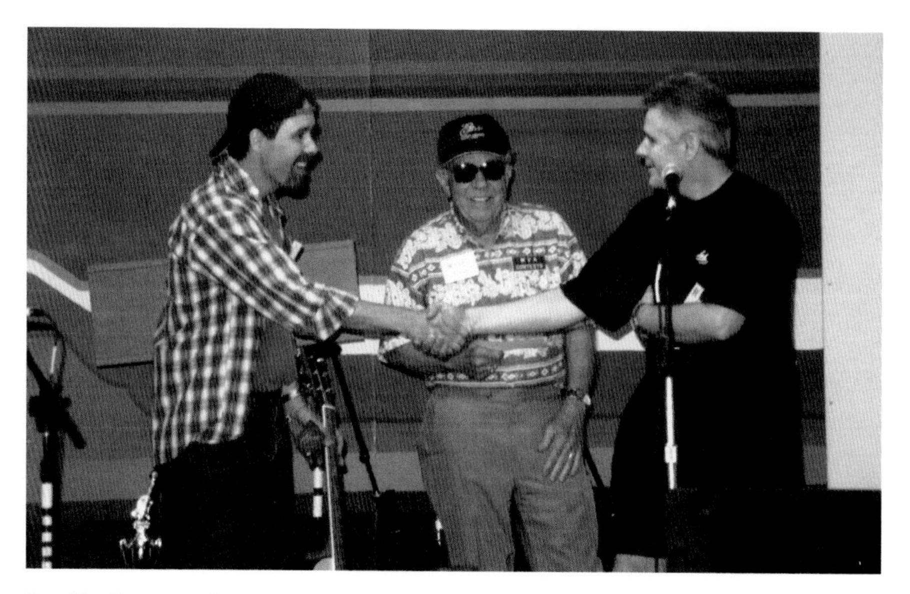

Pete Huttlinger receives a handshake after winning the National Finger Style Guitar Championship in 2000. Contest official Ed Foster (*center*) and Larrivée Guitars representative Larry Lingle offer congratulations. Huttlinger had an extensive career as a solo performer, composer and author. He toured with multiple artists, including John Denver and LeAnn Rimes, and he recorded for guitar innovator Steve Vai's record label. Huttlinger was the contest runner-up in 1999.

media staff who have shared this responsibility. Winners are also given the donating luthier's address so they may send a letter of appreciation. If the winner is unable to take the trophy and instrument home, the prizes are shipped to their home.

After all the stage events are done, the contest coordinators return to the contest trailer. They complete the necessary record keeping and send the list of winners to the information booth, the site office trailer, the media trailer and other locations that need to know who won. Then preparations begin for the next contest.

IMPORTANCE OF THE CONTESTS

According to Rex Flottman, Bob Redford believed that the contests and the quality of the contestants were responsible for the success of the festival, especially because these musicians were among the world's top 5 percent of musicians in their instrument categories. Not only were the contestants interested in learning new techniques, but they also welcomed opportunities to help other musicians get started on their instruments. Redford was convinced that if the contests were eliminated, this type of mentoring would also decrease.

After nearly fifteen years of overseeing the contests, the Fosters believed they were becoming more competitive and even more vital. Newspaper publisher Dave Seaton concurred. He wrote in 2005 that these contests make WVF what it is. And he warned that supporting high-quality contests remained important, because contestants are "moveable.…Their enormous value is hard to calculate. Hanging on to these contests should be a top priority for Winfield."

6
PICKERS PARADISE

By Seth Bate

From the beginning, the Walnut Valley Association was committed to being a musician's festival. Organizers booked performers of the highest caliber, held contests to celebrate instrumental expertise in both new and traditional styles and designed the festival experience around the premise that ticket-buyers would join together to play music. "We wanted to encourage the people who played an instrument," said Kendra Redford, "and that's part of what has contributed to the campgrounds jams, which are a big part of the festival now."

By 1981, if not well before, the efforts to attract musicians as attendees was working. Of the people who answered a survey that year, more than one-third played the guitar and more than 60 percent played an instrument of some kind. Almost three-quarters of the respondents attended an instrument workshop, and two-thirds watched an instrument contest. Most important to the festival's brand, more than 30 percent participated in what the survey called "Parkin' Lot Pickin'." The artists whose names were on the festival poster were approachable in Winfield, and they taught interactive workshops and joined in the campground picking after the stages closed.

RISE OF THE FLAT-PICKERS

By the early 1970s, bluegrass had an audience established and devoted enough to support three monthly publications: *Bluegrass Unlimited*, *Muleskinner News* and *Pickin'*, and there was a related interest in flat-picking. In the first waves of bluegrass bands, the guitar was primarily a rhythm instrument, taking a backseat to the flashier (and louder) mandolin, fiddle and banjo. A guitar player who could keep time and throw in a Lester Flatt G-run—a bit of musical ornamentation that was a signature of Flatt's time in Bill Monroe's band the Blue Grass Boys—here and there was a fine addition to a band.

The 1950s and 1960s folk revival helped guitar players discover Doc Watson, who appeared at several of the high-profile folk festivals. Watson inspired players to rethink what the guitar could accomplish as a solo instrument and in combination with other instruments with his ability to play fiddle tunes such as "Black Mountain Rag" as guitar solos.

In the 1960s and 1970s, however, even guitarists who were attracted to acoustic instruments were influenced by the guitar heroes of rock and blues music, and they wanted their share of attention in bluegrass bands and jams. Guitarists such as Tony Rice, playing with J.D. Crowe and the New South, garnered as much spotlight time as their louder bandmates. The increased recognition of flat-picking as its own guitar style helped set the stage for the WVF. With the right inspiration on stage and the right instruments in hand, aspiring guitarists would have reason to come back to Winfield year after year.

To signal the festival's commitment to musicians and to distinguish itself from other events, the WVA launched the National Flat-Pick Championship. The flat-picking guitar style employed a plectrum—the pick—to play distinct melodies on an acoustic steel-string guitar. Often, the tunes selected were the same tunes a fiddle player might choose to accompany a dance. Sometimes a flat-picker would play the melody simply by picking out single notes, but as the style evolved, accomplished players mixed in ornamentation, harmony notes and strummed chords.

As writer Bob Hamrick noted in his book about the festival, *September's Song*, the contest took top billing for the first year; the weekend event was named the "National Guitar Flat-Picking Championship, Bluegrass Music and Folk Arts and Crafts Festival." The poster from the second year advertised the "Second National Flat-Picking Championship" at the top, followed by the location, dates, a sketch of half a guitar—an early version of what would become one of the festival's logos—and finally "Walnut Valley Bluegrass Festival and Crafts Fair."

The contest idea was luthier Stuart Mossman's contribution. He saw it as a way to elevate the festival's appeal and give it a hook, much like the National Oldtime Fiddle Contest did for a festival in Weiser, Idaho. Mossman also saw the contest as a way to tie the WVF to this emerging style of guitar playing. He and a fellow traveler had been floored by a visit to the Philadelphia Folk Festival, where they saw Norman Blake and Dave Bromberg trading licks. "[M]y interest lay in guitars and good flat-pickers like Doc Watson, Norman Blake and Dan Crary. There was no 'National Bluegrass' anything at the time," Mossman said. "So, we created the National Guitar Flat-Picking Championship." The contest made the Winfield festival unique.

Of course, the concept of a music competition was hardly new. Fairs and festivals around the country had fiddle contests. Nevertheless, the flat-pick championship earned instant prestige. Practitioners and fans of the flat-pick style were a small but rabid subset of guitar geeks, and the chance to earn the notice of Watson, Blake or Crary was a strong motivator. The annual contest contributed to a rapid growth in the abilities contestants displayed. "Have you been to a flat-picking contest lately?" Crary asked in a column he wrote in 1979. "In many ways, they're an amazing experience. At last year's National Flat-Picking Championship Festival at Winfield, Kansas, the field of contestants included at least thirty players who were doing things unheard of ten years ago."

Winfield became a place where the best of the best players could show they belonged in the same company as—and sometimes on the same stages with—the preeminent players of their styles. While flat-picking guitar players all owed something to Doc Watson, bluegrass banjo players were all indebted to Earl Scruggs, who largely defined the bluegrass banjo style in his tenure with the Blue Grass Boys and his own influential band, Flatt and Scruggs and the Foggy Mountain Boys. Scruggs himself never played at WVF, though his immediate successor in the Blue Grass Boys did. Don Reno performed at Winfield in 1975. Bela Fleck, perhaps the foremost banjo player of all time, played at WVF with the 1980s lineup of New Grass Revival.

Bill Monroe himself may have been the biggest influence on bluegrass mandolin players, though plenty of players were in awe of Sam Bush, the mandolin player who anchored New Grass Revival; New Grass played at WVF eleven times from 1972 to 1989.

New Grass Revival in an official Walnut Valley Festival promotional photograph from 1977. *Clockwise from top left*: Courtney Johnson (banjo), John Cowan (electric bass), Curtis Burch (guitar) and Sam Bush (mandolin).

Left: Sam Bush grins through a fiddle solo in 1989. The inclusion of Bush's band, New Grass Revival, at the first Walnut Valley Festival demonstrated that Winfield was a place for both traditional and progressive bluegrass. Among the eleven years New Grass played Winfield were 1972 (its first year playing as a band) and 1989 (its final year playing as a band).

Right: Banjo legend Bela Fleck plays with New Grass Revival in 1987. Fleck is a two-time International Bluegrass Music Association Award winner, a fourteen-time Grammy Award winner and a member of the American Banjo Hall of Fame.

Fingerstyle guitar players represent an even wider blend of techniques and musical genres than flat-pickers. Even so, they all have some link back to Merle Travis and one of his successors, Chet Atkins. Atkins, a guitar player and music producer, perfected the technique of using the thumb to pluck out a bass accompaniment and the remaining fingers to play melody and other harmonies. Atkins never played WVF, but Travis performed in 1976 at the Walnut Valley Spring Thing. Tommy Emmanuel, one of only five players to receive the official version of the Chet Atkins "Certified Guitar Player" designation, was featured at WVF eight times starting in 2000. Muriel Anderson, another favorite of Atkins, won the National Finger Pick Guitar Championship in 1989 and returned as a performer in 2019.

Aside from traditional bluegrass instruments, the WVF prominently featured world-class performers on other acoustic instruments. The

Left: New Grass Revival lead singer and bass player John Cowan performs in 1987. The 1980s lineup of the progressive bluegrass group had several songs on the country *Billboard* charts, including the top-forty hit "Callin' Baton Rouge" in 1989.

Below: Two guitar innovators, Doc Watson (*left*) and Merle Travis (*right*), jam backstage at the Spring Thing in 1976. Watson was an inspiration to generations of flat-pickers. Travis was such an influence on fingerpickers that his signature way of alternating bass notes while fingerpicking is known universally as "Travis picking." Travis was inducted into the Country Music Hall of Fame in 1977.

Right: Tommy Emmanuel stands at the lip of the stage to deliver a typically exuberant performance in 2003. Early in his career, the Australian Emmanuel played with rock acts, including Air Supply. Inspired by players like his hero Chet Atkins, Emmanuel switched to acoustic guitar. In eight Winfield appearances, Emmanuel frequently shared the stage with Stephen Bennett.

Below: Hammer dulcimer player Walt Michael is joined by John McCutcheon for a four-handed duet in 1988 as audience members dance in front of the stage.

Left: Mountain dulcimer virtuoso David Schnaufer plays on Stage II in 1991. The champion of the first National Mountain Dulcimer Contest, Schnaufer, was a performer, student and professor of the instrument. He appeared on recordings by Emmylou Harris, Johnny Cash, Mark O'Connor and his dulcimer student Cyndi Lauper. Schnaufer died in 2006.

Right: Bryan Bowers displays his mastery of the autoharp in 1989. Bowers first performed at Walnut Valley in 1975. His humorous songs and stories were so popular in the 1970s that festival organizers sometimes worried that his crowd would get out of control and mar the festival's family-friendly environment. Bowers was the first modern autoharp virtuoso, and he was the first living person inducted into the Autoharp Hall of Fame.

unexpected rise in popularity of the hammer dulcimer helped the festival capture and keep audiences. "In the early years, there was a hammer dulcimer player who came to the festival by the name of Cathy Barton who just took our crowd by storm because nobody had ever seen the instrument before, and nobody had seen anybody play like that. Cathy Barton and her husband now, Dave Para, have been regulars to the festival over the years," Kendra Redford said. A college senior at her first festival, Barton was a favorite workshop presenter. Aside from the hammer dulcimer, she played the clawhammer banjo, the mountain dulcimer, the autoharp and "found" instruments, such as bones and spoons.

The autoharp, an instrument associated with country music pioneers the Carter Family, has had a contest at Winfield since 1981. Bryan Bowers, who

Mountain dulcimer player Bing Futch shines on Stage II in 2018. Reflecting afterward, Futch wrote, "It's people that truly make this festival what it is, and their collective ownership of this festival is part of what makes it so great. I'm not one to blow smoke... but I don't mince words in saying that this is the best festival that I've ever had the pleasure of attending. It's unlike anything else that I've ever experienced, and it is a nonstop rush of goodness."

redefined the instrument, has appeared as a festival performer eighteen times. Along with Bowers, at least three Winfield winners are also members of the Mountain Laurel Autoharp Hall of Fame: Lucille Reilly, Les Gustafson-Zook and Winfield native Karen Mueller.

LEGENDARY JAMS

Tut Taylor, an innovative Dobro player and music entrepreneur, might have been the first person to call Winfield, Kansas, "Pickers Paradise." In 1976, Taylor told organizers that at their events, the pickin' by amateurs under the trees and beneath the grandstand was as good as the pickin' by professionals on the stage. Art Coats said he would start using the alliterative phrase. (Taylor also created the WVA Lyre logo that is still used in some communication.)

While the contests showcased individual virtuosity, the spirit of Winfield emerged in collaboration. Instrumental jams gave pickers the opportunity to take turns playing variations of a melody, often a traditional fiddle tune. When not playing the lead, the players strummed chords, often using the "bluegrass chop," a percussive accompaniment most associated with the mandolin. These jams took place throughout the campground and parking lots. When they were on stage, though, they sometimes became the stuff of legend.

The Walnut Valley Festival established its identity with one of those jams in 1972. *Pickin'* carried a photograph of "the now famous three-guitar jam session" with Blake, Crary and Watson, three flat-pickers trading tunes. Without banjos and basses to mask the voices of guitars, the players brought out the best in each other. The following year, Clarence White was booked to play the festival and join an encore of the jam, but he was killed in an accident with a drunk driver. Tony Rice took his place. Facilitating these "meetings of the fingers" became a point of pride for the festival.

More innovative pairings followed. Promotions director Art Coats hyped a three-Dobro jam featuring Blake, Tut Taylor and Curtis Burch. Leota Coats remembered, "Art had really a gift at putting musicians together that hadn't played together before, and then there would be kind of this magic

Luthier and Dobro player Tut Taylor might have been the first person to call Winfield, Kansas, "Pickers Paradise." In 1976, he told publicist Art Coats that the picking in the campground and under the grandstand was as good as the playing on stage. The National Tut Taylor Dobro Championship was the headline event of the one and only Walnut Valley Spring Thing Festival.

Fiddler Gary Hughes gives a nod to the next picker during a daytime jam at Scamp Camp in 2003. Some of the other players included Bill Lisk, Deanna Lisk, Paula Shearheart (hammer dulcimer), Georgia Hughes and Mike Shields.

A campground jam in 2012 included past Finger Style Guitar Championship winner Rolly Brown (*holding fiddle*) and Tim May (*center*), who has appeared on WVF stages in bands such as Crucial Smith and Plaidgrass.

Elkin Thomas (*left*) emcees, as Larry Booth (*right*) of Colby, Kansas, prepares to sing his winning entry in the 1987 edition of the NewSong Showcase. The songwriters' showcase, started in part at the urging of Wayne Steadham, has helped foster a community of songwriters at the festival. Over the years, it has been coordinated and hosted by Aileen and Elkin Thomas (1987–93), Crow Johnson (1994–2003), Donna Stjerna and Kelly Mulholland (2004–19), and Chris Jones (2020–present). In 2001, Seth Bate stepped in to host a set.

on stage." In 1975, a twin banjo set matched Don Reno with Mike Lilly, then playing in the Lonesome Ramblers, a band led by singer and guitarist Larry Sparks.

The life cycle of bands also meant seeing high-caliber artists in different lineups over the years. For example, a festival stalwart beginning in 1972 was Byron Berline, a fiddle player who had toured in Bill Monroe's band, the Blue Grass Boys, and a California session musician who played in the Flying Burrito Brothers. Perhaps best known in the bluegrass world as the founder of the Country Gazette, Berline returned to WVF over the years in a dizzying number of acts, including Sundance, BCH (Berline, Crary and Hickman), California and the Byron Berline Band. He was often joined onstage by his nephew Barry "Bones" Patton. Patton's proficiency with the rhythm sticks was legendary, and in 2019, he won the International Bone Playing Competition in Ireland.

With campgrounds and parking lots full of happy musicians, tents full of stressed-out contest entrants and stages full of premier players, the annual event lived out its commitment to being a musicians' festival.

In a fitting tribute, a song about the festival environment was written by participant Mikel Steven and was incorporated into a "Walnut Valley Medley" by longtime festival entertainers Aileen and Elkin Thomas:

Down in Walnut Valley, playin' on that guitar,
It's a bluegrass heaven, music from the stars.
Down in Walnut Valley, strummin' on the old banjo,
It's a Picker's Paradise, and everyone's in the show.

7

STAGE 5

By Russell and Sherry Brace

A beloved Walnut Valley Festival tradition is Stage 5, the officially unofficial campground stage. (Festival tradition is to reference the official interior stages with Roman numerals I, II, III and IV, while unofficial campground stages, such as 5, 6, 7, and 11, use Arabic numerals.) Campground pickers of all styles sign up for slots to perform on Stage 5, and its late-night crowds often rival those of the fairground stages in numbers and enthusiasm. Some of the artists hired by WVA also get invited to play Stage 5, blurring the line between professional musicians and amateur enthusiasts.

It was a cold and snowy day in the winter of 1986. Russell Brace and two of his friends were headed south from Wichita to Mulvane, Kansas, to pick up his new purchase—a 1954 Chevrolet 4100 one-and-a-half-ton flatbed farm truck, complete with stake sides and cattle racks. The roads were slick and icy, but the trip back to Wichita was successful. It was an unusual sight to see this old farm truck motoring through the modern streets of Wichita, but it was Russell's only transportation.

Naturally, as September rolled around, Russell loaded up the old truck and headed south again, this time to his annual vacation site, the National Flat-Pick Championships in Winfield, Kansas. There, Russell met up with campmates Bob Ennis and Steve Keen in the Pecan Grove for a week of music, fun and friends. Another campmate, Sherry Merry, arrived later in the week.

While sitting around the campfire, Russell mentioned to Bob and Steve, "We should build a stage on the back of the old truck." After some discussion, they devised a plan and came up with a list of needed supplies. The boys headed off to the local Winfield lumber yard, forgetting the supply list. They quickly re-created it, purchased the supplies and headed back to the Pecan Grove to begin their work on the stage.

After two days of intense construction, using a few hundred feet of rope, an old tarp and a cobbled-together set of steps, the stage was complete but lacked a name. Since the midway boasted four stages, Russell sat down with an old piece of plywood, a can of paint and brushed the words "Stage 5."

The boys were just putting the finishing touches on the stage when Sherry arrived at the camp. Sherry had provided a banner to hang so she could find the camp when she arrived. The banner, which read "Hopelessly Lost at C," was hung prominently above the stage. The new stage was oriented among the tents and faced north toward Fourteenth Avenue.

When Bob Redford saw Stage 5 for the first time, the wheels immediately started turning. He needed a stage at the Wheeler IGA grocery store for a promotional event. He asked if he could borrow it for the afternoon and promised to return it to the Pecan Grove exactly as he found it when the event was over. Redford sent a crew to prepare the truck for transport, and with Russell at the wheel and a police escort, Stage 5 drove down Main Street to the store's parking lot. Walt Michael and Company and the Hopelessly Lost at C Band played on the stage. Festival entertainers Aileen and Elkin Thomas danced in the parking lot as Hopelessly Lost at C played their tune "Come Alive, Country Lady."

A campground stage for amateur musicians to perform on at the Winfield Festival was unheard of, and it became clear that just building a stage would not be enough to guarantee performers. The Stage 5 crew resorted to bribing bands with homemade peach cobbler and hand-churned ice cream for sharing a few songs on the stage. By festival's end, however, it was obvious that the new stage was a hit. The Stage 5 Camp was honored in 1987 and 1988 with the Best Campsite Contest Award. In 1989, from Stage I on Saturday night, Bob Redford presented the Stage 5 crew with an official festival sign.

The stage's appearance has evolved over the years. The "Hopelessly Lost at C" theme was developed into the look of an old sailing ship, with flags, sails, an anchor (with a G-clef incorporated into it) and lots of other nautical regalia. During this time, "unplugged" music came to prominence, so the crew added a new banner/sail that read "Stage 5: Cut Adrift." In 2007, after

A performer demonstrates a bowed psaltery during one of the daytime slots on Stage 5 in 1995. Campground jammers and other artists sign up to perform on Stage 5. Other homegrown stages followed, but Stage 5 was the first to receive "officially unofficial" status.

being the "Hopelessly Lost at C" Ship for twenty years, Stage 5 became a Gypsy wagon, reflecting the spirit, diversity and personality of its expanded crew. The Stage 5 Motel design appeared in 2011, the camp's twenty-fifth year, complete with retro motel key fobs, individual soaps, "Do Not Disturb" door hangers and stickers that said, "Stage 5 Motel….More than just a one-mic stand."

Over the past thirty-five years, Stage 5 has grown and adapted in many different ways. Aside from the physical look of the stage, the way that the sound is reproduced evolved from a totally acoustic venue to the Acoustic Instrument Megaphones (AIM), designed by Steve Keen, to full-blown mics, monitors and large stacks of speakers, even to the two-microphone/surround-sound system that is currently in use. Other evolutions include the handling of signing up for a time slot, the length of the time slot, the daily schedule, the hours of operation and the construction of the stage.

One thing that has remained the same—with the exception of the first year—is Stage 5 souvenir picks. Every September, the Stage 5 crew gives away hundreds of them with a unique design or color scheme each year.
An undertaking like a campground stage requires a hardworking and

Linda Cunningham, Dee Dunlap Van Boening and Barney Byard play on Stage 5 in 2003. Acts on Stage 5 range from beginners to internationally touring headliners. The stage was first set up on the back of a 1954 Chevrolet 4100 flatbed farm truck in 1987.

dedicated crew. Stage 5 has been blessed with great friends who have volunteered. Their largest reward is knowing that their actions helped someone else have a fun experience at the festival. The assembled crew comes from Kansas, Oklahoma and Texas. The crew has a heart for the mission of Stage 5 and a passion for acoustic music.

From its beginning, Stage 5 has been overwhelmed with a generous amount of spontaneous help from folks who camp nearby. In retrospect, a manual for how to build and operate a campground stage would have been very handy.

The stage has given festivalgoers so many memorable moments, so many wonderful people and unsurpassed musicianship, weddings, memorials and funny and poignant songs. Festivalgoers shared a stunned silence on September 11, 2001; then in remembrance and solidarity, they passed an enormous American flag through the Stage 5 crowd while singing "God Bless America." Hearing a favorite performer, experiencing a new favorite performer, seeing friends that you only see in September at the festival, attending a golf cart drive-in movie, learning a new tune, playing an old

Right: The morning after winning the International Finger Style Championship in 2017, Christie Lenée opened Stage 5. Contest winners and booked entertainers at the festival are also often regulars on campground stages and at campsite jams. *Seth Bate.*

Below: The Wilders exchange grins in 2004. The high-energy old-time and honkytonk band played in Winfield eleven times in twelve festivals, beginning in 2000. Their Stage 5 sets sometimes drew a bigger crowd than their official stage performances. *From left to right*: The band's members were Betse Ellis (fiddle), Nate Gawron (bass), Ike Sheldon (guitar) and Phil Wade (dobro).

fiddle tune, laughing, crying, hugging and bidding sad farewell at the end of a weeklong gathering all make for a treasure trove of memories. These are not exclusive to Stage 5 but extend to every camp at Winfield—the vibe of friendship, peace and love brought together by the love of music.

Throughout the years, Stage 5 has hosted hundreds of hours of live music and many different types of acoustic music. Stage 5 has even been the catalyst for (and sometimes topic of) original music. Professional, amateur and even beginner musicians have graced the hallowed wood of the old wheat truck's bed. The notes and sounds shared there have permeated the souls of the people who come to Stage 5 to play and listen alike.

8

THE PECULIAR ADVENTURES OF THE DONUT TRACTORS

By Poppin' Johnnies

Each year, the members of the Winfield Masonic Lodge No. 110 drive tractors pulling coffee trailers throughout the campgrounds, selling coffee and donuts as a fundraiser. The event is called the "Poppin' Johnny Coffee Run," and it has given lodge members an up-close look at morning camp life.

The One-Hundred-Dollar Cup of Coffee

At least once a year, an anonymous camper will use a one-hundred-dollar bill to pay for a cup of coffee. When offered change, the camper's response will be, "Keep it. I know what good works you do." Sometimes, the response will be, "Please donate that to the Shriners' Hospital for Children." We are thankful for the generous support of this unknown bluegrass fan.

—Jim Stevens

The Girl in the Hammock

Once during the Poppin' Johnny Coffee Run, as a tractor was being hailed for a donut, one of the Masons observed a girl in a hammock just waking up from what was apparently a fine night of partying. Looking extremely

Top: Campers line up for showers in 1983. Through the years, the WVA has partnered with vendors to provide showers in the campground and with community entities, such as the Winfield Recreation Commission, to provide showers in the community.

Bottom: Experienced campers learn that many items can serve multiple functions, which leaves room for more instruments and food. Why pack a shaving mirror when there is already a mirror on your vehicle (1987)?

Opposite: A teenage Kacey Musgraves yodels on a campground stage in 2003. The festival stages, camps and contests have been important in the development of many young artists, including some who became stars. Within ten years of her Winfield appearance, Musgraves was a nationally touring act recording for Mercury Nashville. From there, she went on to release four top five *Billboard* albums.

disheveled, disoriented and obviously in a miserable state of mind, she rose to a sitting position on the edge of the hammock and assessed her condition. Looking first at her shirt, she exclaimed, "This isn't my shirt!" Hopping from the hammock, she looked down at her feet. One foot was bare, and the other was clad in a tennis shoe. A baffled look crossed her face as she continued, "And that's not my tennis shoe!"

—anonymous lodge member

Wildlife Escapades on the Walnut River

The coffee run coordinator fielded a complaint one year that the tractors were spending too much time servicing the lower roads by the river and neglecting the upper roads close to Fourteenth Avenue. During the investigation, the coordinator discovered that the tractor drivers and crew were ogling skinny dippers enjoying a swim in the Walnut River. Thankfully, the Masons were only observers and not participators. We do have an image to uphold.

—Fred Miller

Vintage Tractor vs. Nice Pickup

Four or five years ago, Winfield Mason Danny Uden had an incident while driving one of the tractors that led to an unexpected friendship. Uden was getting too close to a nice 1980s pickup and decided he needed to take evasive action. He hit the brake, thinking it was the clutch, but failed to slow the tractor's powerful engine. He was in a panic when he finally pulled the clutch handle, but it was too late. The tractor came to a stop a fraction of a second after smearing mud on the bumper of the pickup.

Guitars, a banjo, a dulcimer and a baby are all part of this jam circle in front of a campground tepee in 1977.

Dumbfounded that he could make such a lame-brained mistake, Uden immediately found the owner to inform him of the incident. The forgiving pickup owner told the tractor driver not to worry about it. Every year since, Uden made it a point to meet up with the pickup owner each morning of the festival to supply him with a cup of coffee—free of charge.

—Danny Uden

9
WINFIELD MEMORIES

By Tim Sidebottom

In nearly forty years as part of the festival crew, Tim Sidebottom has seen it all. The following are just a few of his stories about festival operations, campground culture and the relationship between the crew and the performers.

Flood Rush

One year, we had lined up all the campers waiting for the line rush in the west campground, but the river pushed our schedule up by two days, as it was raining in Winfield and, more importantly, upstream. With great slipping, creative vocabulary and lots of muddy boots and clothes, we helped all the campers on the low road and the first line above the low road to move up to the blacktop. Rick Meyer even managed to keep the campers in order when some tried to take advantage of the situation to make spots for their friends.

The remaining tents and such were moved by the staff with the call of "Hey, drop everything, grab a truck with an empty bed or trailer and follow us." The river ultimately covered only the low road, but it could have just as easily come up another five feet.

Weather shapes each year's festival experience, and the same river that makes the Winfield Fairground a picturesque spot for camping also sometimes makes camping treacherous. In 1993, a canoe was the best way to get through a low spot after a flash flood. In 2008 and 2016, flooding caused organizers to close the campground, and campers were redirected to nearby spots, such as Winfield City Lake and the Napawalla Campground in Oxford.

"HEY, DID YOU KNOW YOUR PORT-A-POT IS ON FIRE?"

Late one Sunday afternoon, the Boy Scouts were picking up trash barrels in the Pecan Grove as Ron Deal and I were in the office trailer deciding where we might get supper and celebrate the end of another festival. The scout leader called Rick Meyer on the two-way and asked, "Hey Rick, did you know one of your port-a-pots is on fire?" One of us asked "Where at?" The leader said by pole B-11.

Ron and I grabbed two fire extinguishers from the trailer and jumped into my truck to speed down to the grove. The trouble spot was obvious as we turned onto Fourteenth Avenue, and I cut across the empty campground, dodging piles of unused firewood and bags of trash. Ron yanked the door open, and I fired the extinguisher into the flames through the smoke. Most of the fire was out, but some melting plastic from the urinal tube was still dripping down from a flame under the edge. Two more shots of white powder, and the pot was out—but not useable. We turned it toward a tree and later moved it off with a forklift. I don't think we ever moved so fast—except maybe for ice cream and cobbler.

The Memorial Jar

One year, I was talking to three others in the office trailer when we heard—and more to the point, felt—a *boom*. Jerry O'Neil said it was only a backfire, but the way the ground moved, I thought different. As we opened the door, the radio went off. Security announced that a camper in the west campground had blown up. We all headed out to help, but after seeing the roof laying on four blown-out walls and that security had it covered, we went back to getting the festival up and running.

The most memorable thing about this event was not the explosion or that the lady injured in the blast seemed to be getting better later that week, but rather that a one-gallon glass jar was placed on the ground in front of where her camper had been with a note asking for donations to aid in her recovery. The simple jar remained in the same spot for five days. There was no chain holding it down, no one standing guard, no security cameras. But that jar filled with cash during the week, and no one even considered taking it. Winfield campers are what humanity should be—or could be if we tried.

Bobby Redford's Walnut Valley Band

One year, John McCutcheon and Tom Chapin were on Stage I and announced that they were Bobby Redford's Walnut Valley Band as they did a parody of "Sergeant Pepper's Lonely Hearts Club Band."

The next year, just after they finished their sound check on Stage I, Ron Deal and Tim Sidebottom scurried across the back of the stage and hung a large sign on previously installed hanging hooks that boldly read, "BOBBY REDFORD'S WALNUT VALLEY BAND." The crowd screamed its approval, and both entertainers were lost for words as the culprits scurried back off stage.

BURY ME ON STAGE III

Tom Chapin penned a note to WVA staff and to Bob and Kendra Redford about his love for Stage III. The audience being only three feet away made it seem like a large group of friends around a campfire. As far as Chapin was concerned, he said, "You can bury me on Stage III."

A surprise was waiting for Tom the next year, created with the cooperation of Bill Barwick, Roz Brown and the band Bluestem. As Bill introduced Tom to the crowd, he pulled out a copy of the letter and explained to the crowd what it said. Bluestem, wearing full duster coats and black hats, then brought out a coffin and a tombstone with Tom's name on it. They stood the coffin up on end and had Tom step back into it then laid him down and moved him off stage a short space. Finally, they tipped it back up and let him out.

The last thing heard as the pranksters left the stage was, "Wait for next year and the resurrection!"

Bill Barwick (*left*) and Roz Brown (*center*) welcome Michael Martin Murphey to a set of cowboy songs and stories on Stage IV in 2011. Brown started performing and emceeing at Winfield in 1983. His frequent performing partner from Denver's Buckhorn Exchange, Barwick, began his association with Winfield about a decade later. Many Winfield artists over the years have been recognized by the International Western Music Association, including Barwick, Murphey, Juni Fisher, Dave Stamey, Prickly Pair and the Cactus Chorale, Don Edwards and Barry Ward.

Free to Lay

One year, a group brought a converted Frito-Lay truck as a camper and set it up in the Pecan Grove. A closer look at the logo showed that it actually said Free to Lay. The truck was in fact a mobile bar complete with a sound system, lights, a dance pole and even a small back room where the girls could do extra favors for anyone who paid for them.

It was not long before word about the truck made it to the festival staff, and with the help of the Winfield Police Department, festival security closed the operation for violating the festival's policy that prohibited the "sale of items or services within the campgrounds without the written permission of [crafts director] Paulette Rush." The vehicle was impounded, and the girls and manager were held in jail on various prostitution charges.

The police were gone and security was arranging for the tow of the vehicle when a car pulled up with four more girls dressed rather scantily. They turned out to be the next shift coming in, so they also were redirected to the jail. One of the girls involved seemed very put out and said the truck had been operating at the state fair for two weeks and that no one up there had a problem with them.

The Queen of Entrances

For two days running, performers Tom Chapin and John McCutcheon had given sign artist Linda Tilton grief about a tight black bustier she had said she would wear for them on Saturday. Early Saturday afternoon, Linda headed back from the festival ground to her motel to get ready, but she couldn't find her keys. Someone gave her a ride to the motel, but her room key was on the ring with her car keys. The manager allowed her into the room, but she was running late.

After changing, Linda was heading back to the fairgrounds and called Steve Hyle from the security crew to see if they could get her to the back of Stage I without having to stop at the security checkpoint. Festival artists are issued special keychains that serve as their all-access passes, and Linda's was on her missing key ring. Steve took to the idea as most staff do—by going all out.

A five-car escort, complete with red lights and sirens, met Linda at the gate and took her all the way to the backstage area, where the audience could clearly see her arrival. John and Tom had to bow to the "queen of entrances" as they started playing and Linda joined them onstage. (The keys were found on a metal bleacher on the track in front of Stage I.)

Honeymoon in the Pecan Grove

There have been many honeymoons in the campgrounds, including that of one couple who came directly from the church to the Pecan Grove. The bride was doing quite well in her heels and long veil, and the groom was trying to not get too much mud on his shiny, slick Oxfords. Their camp group had everything ready for them and gave them privacy (as much as can be had in a festival) and didn't wake them up too early.

SS *Feisty*

One year, Bob Redford was convinced people were crossing the river into the campground to avoid buying a wristband. He purchased a small sailboat with a motor to patrol the Walnut River with a high-beam flashlight. We dubbed it the SS *Feisty*.

Bob asked me to try to put together a ping-pong ball gun with air pressure power to tag any offenders we spotted with a dye pack of some sort. After some discussion, we concluded we did not have the crew to run the boat or time to reinvent the paintball gun. The idea went on the shelf—literally—in the festival's warehouse.

We don't think river crossing was actually much of a problem, but the rumor mill about the patrol boat started. It probably stopped the timid from trying, so the SS *Feisty* served a purpose, even if it never got on the water.

"I Need My Sleep!"

On a Tuesday or Wednesday morning, bright and early, a camper approached the ticket trailer staff and demanded that they stop all this music being played by his campsite: "They played music almost all night, and I need my sleep!"

Above: Eddy Poindexter paints a stage backdrop in 1989. Poindexter, known for making hand-painted advertisement road signs for years, came to Winfield to be close to family. He offered to hand paint original stage backgrounds for WVA over several years. Bob Redford suggested designs, and Poindexter brought them to life.

Right: Steve Fry of Elk Falls Pottery displays a giant souvenir mug in 2004. Purchasing a handmade mug by Steve and Jane Fry has been a tradition for many festivalgoers since 1981. Steve and Jane were inspired to build their pottery business as students at Hesston College in the 1970s.

We asked if it was his first festival, and when he said yes, we suggested to the "Winfield virgin" some tamer camp locations. Still, we told him, "It's a music festival for musicians. They will only get louder and later until Sunday night." We also suggested he could camp ten miles away at the Winfield City Lake, which is what I think he finally did.

10

THE *WALNUT VALLEY VOICE*

By Larry Junker

One of the challenges of an instant community like the one that comes to the Walnut Valley Festival is how to spread information. Whether it's the name of the latest contest winner, the lineup for a campground stage or an emergency announcement, it is hard to spread news consistently.

Naturally, there are grassroots sources of information, such as bulletin boards, fliers on portable toilets and the ever-circulating rumor mill. Online listservs like the Winfield-l and social media groups, such as the Walnut Valley Bluegrass Festival Fans Facebook group, are run by fans. The WVA's official on-site communication channels during each year's festival include the program, the campground radio station, announcements from the stages and, in recent years, a smartphone app. Perhaps the most recognizable information source is a daily one-sheet newsletter that includes reliable news along with snippets of camp life and community contributions. Its editor is Larry Junker.

The newsletter was first published during the 1996 festival, the twenty-fifth anniversary. Rex Flottman, a media spokesman, shared the Saturday and Sunday editions with me during the summer of 1998. I had been conducting the interviews of the winners of the eight contests since the early 1990s and writing the stories that appeared in the festival's promotional mailing, the *December Occasional.* Rex was using a printer outside of Winfield and having some problems getting the newsletter printed.

Notes on a bulletin board, 1982. Pagers, then cellphones, then WiFi on the festival grounds have all made it easier for festivalgoers to communicate and coordinate, but notes and flyers on bulletin boards and portable toilet doors are still effective.

I said printing this eight-and-a-half-by-fourteen-inch newsletter really was not a problem. Trinity Lutheran Church of Winfield had a printer called a RISO Graph. It could print up to 130 copies per minute. I said that if we could convince Trinity Lutheran to let us use this printer, perhaps we could resurrect the *Walnut Valley Association Voice*, usually shortened to *WVA Voice*. Trinity said sure, and we gave the pastor and his wife tickets to the festival for the use of the printer. That was easy, because I am a member of Trinity.

The *WVA Voice* goes to print most evenings during the festival around midnight, so the next day's issue is available by 8:00 the next morning. And by 8:05 a.m., there is a line of festivalgoers outside the information booth, waiting for their copy.

That first year, 1998, we published eight issues. It started with an issue for Labor Day, welcoming the early arrivers with the idea "to keep attendees up to date with changes in the schedule, contest winners, tidbits of trivial information and etc., etc., etc." The next issue that year was the "Special Land Rush" edition. It was published the day after Land Rush, the official opening of the campground, and on the backside was printed the full four-day schedule. That was immediately a big hit with festivalgoers, as they could fold up the *WVA Voice*, put it in their pocket and refer to it throughout the week. This saved them from taking out the schedule in the center section of the official program; these programs are saved by many as keepsake souvenirs. The *WVA Voice* became an immediate hit because it was just a piece of paper that could be discarded. (In later years, we did find out that some people save the *WVA Voice*, too.)

The lead story of the first Thursday edition proclaimed that the twenty-seventh annual festival was underway with the "Round Em Up" set on Stage III featuring Roz Brown and Bill Barwick. Another story was about a new hot young group called Pagosa Hot Strings. They were just kids, ages fourteen, thirteen and eleven. Also introduced in this issue was the talent and costume contest hosted by the Riverats Camp out in their campsite in the Pecan Grove. This annual contest is still going strong more than twenty years later.

Another feature that started that year in the *Voice* was the Stage 5 schedule for Friday and Saturday. That became another reason readers sought the *Voice* out. With the exception of one year, the schedule for Stage 5 has appeared in every volume since.

The rest of the articles in the *WVA Voice* that year also set the tone for future years. There were short articles on the winners of the various contests. The Sunday edition's back page became a thank-you to all, both attendees and entertainers, for a great festival. And there was a note about filling out the questionnaire that can be found in the festival program, which helps festival personnel plan for the next year.

In conversation with Rex Flottman, I told him that we had created a monster and that we'd better not stop. Rex agreed and then told me the only way I would get out of the job of being publisher, editor and printer of the *Voice* was to die. I'm still at it, and I say, "Lord willing and the creek don't rise," I'll be at it for a few more years.

Over the years, I have had the help of other writers, including Ernie and Patti Hill, Ned Graham, Tom Eckard, Ginger Thomas and others. I have appreciated their help, as we brought festivalgoers stories from the campground.

The following are some insights and memorable stories captured in the *Walnut Valley Voice* over the years.

Bluegrass from France

While delivering the *WVA Voice* out in the Pecan Grove in 2015, I met Pierre Bastide from Paris, France. He has come every year he was able since 2004, when his friend entered the flat-pick contest. The friend had asked Pierre if he would like to go, even though there was no dobro contest. Pierre said that was OK; he'd just come and jam. Needless to say, he was hooked. He is the operations manager for a small festival on the border of France and Switzerland. Pierre loves the idea that he can go from jam to jam to play different kinds of music—the blues, gospel, Beatles and bluegrass.

Feisty's Treasure Hunt

In 2017, the increasing use of technology to enhance the festival experience resulted in Feisty's Treasure Hunt. The Walnut Valley Festival app gave hunters clues to figure out where to go to find a QR code and solve a puzzle. Successful players were instructed to bring their phones to the information booth and show one of the workers there. The first twenty-five people to solve the puzzle received a vintage WVA T-shirt and were entered into a drawing for a Farita guitar designed and provided by Elderly Instruments. The first one hundred finishers got a commemorative Feisty Treasure Hunt pick.

In 2018, there were both junior and adult versions of Feisty's Treasure Hunt. The adult version was trickier to solve, so only a few groups ultimately solved the puzzle.

In Memoriam

The *WVA Voice* has been one place to note the passing of festival family members—staff members, entertainers and campers—over the years. In 2014, the *Voice* put out an "extra" to highlight those festival workers and friends who had died in the past year. The issue named Paul Doolittle, Perl Ruggles and Phil Schmidt, who had all worked the ticket trailer at the main gate; Rick Marshal, a volunteer EMT; Art Charlet of the Stage 5 crew; Frank Johnson, the director of the Winfield City Band; Royce McSpadden,

Singer-songwriter Sean Della Croce plays a song in tribute to her late stepdad, Pete Huttlinger, on Stage II in 2016. Among the full stage of musicians who gathered to remember Huttlinger were Andy May, Stephen Bennett, Helen Avakian, Brian Henke and Todd Hallawell.

the founder of McSpadden Dulcimer Co.; and Ron Deal, a crew chief and manager of the festival stages and signs.

In 2018, the newsletter reported the loss of a couple of stalwarts of the staff. In February 2018, Paulette Rush, a longtime organizer of the Arts and Crafts Show, passed away. And just a week or so before the 2018 event, crew chief Larry Hittle passed away. He was instrumental in helping get the grounds ready for festivalgoers.

In addition to important people, the *WVA Voice* has sometimes marked the passing of landmarks. In 2018, the newsletter highlighted the art on the festival poster. It depicted the distinctive West Fourteenth Avenue Bridge, which for safety reasons was demolished to make way for a new bridge spanning the Walnut River.

The old bridge was used as a secondary entrance to the grounds during the festival, with a gate staffed by crew members located on the east side. For quite a few patrons, the bridge served as the gateway for their final departure from festival grounds each year.

Rex Flottman said, "Through the years, people crossed over the West Fourteenth Bridge to discover an entirely new world, a world of music—music that was being performed, shared, taught and experienced for decades.

Now, the old iron bridge is gone, replaced by a new, modern concrete bridge, and I wonder what new music the next generation of travelers crossing over the bridge into our community will bring with them to share."

MUSIC CAMP FOR KIDS

From the early days, the WVA has looked for ways to include families and connect them to music. In 2018, the *WVA Voice* announced a new experience designed specifically for kids. Dubbed the Feisty Music Camp for Kids, the two-day event gave children the chance to take part in hands-on, music-related crafts, workshops and concerts. Music Camp codirectors Erin Mae and Peter Thomas Lague organized and operated the camp, drawing on a wealth of experience.

Stage 6, a campground stage that has hosted some of the best players in the world at its legendary all-night jam sessions over the years, agreed to host the camp for children (preschoolers to sixth graders) on Friday and Saturday afternoon. This was not a drop-off event; parents or guardians were expected to remain onsite to observe the excitement firsthand. The Feisty Kids Camp has returned every year since.

WALNUT VALLEY ROCKS

Another festival tradition documented by the *WVA Voice* was Rockin' Walnut Valley. A group of people—more than one hundred rock painters—pooled their efforts to paint rocks. Nancy Parrot, one of the leaders in this movement, told the *Voice*, "Welcome rock painters! Let's have some fun with our rocks at the Walnut Valley Festival!"

The artists planned to paint some rocks and hide or strategically place them on the festival grounds and in the campgrounds. Anyone who found a rock was requested to please share a picture of it on the Rockin' Walnut Valley Facebook page. The finders were welcome to keep theirs rocks or hide them again.

Camp Glo-Vegetable, located in the campground just north of Fourteenth Avenue, also hosted anyone who wanted to paint a rock. Commonly used media for the rocks were pencil, colored pencil, oil pastels, Sharpie markers and crayons. Clear spray paint was used to protect the decoration.

Campsite Origins and Anniversaries

The geography of the festival campground changes each year. It would be difficult to document even a fraction of the campsites. Many of them have names, decorations, traditions and even public events of their own. Each year, the *WVA Voice* spotlights a few of the camps.

In 2019, the *Voice* wished a happy thirty-fourth anniversary to Carp Camp. The West Campground fixture known for its giant jam sessions that attract the highest caliber players started out as "Gathering in the Grass." When someone brought a T-shirt from Minnesota with a carp on it, the group thereafter became famously known as Carp Camp.

The same year, Stillwater Camp was marking its forty-fourth (or so) anniversary. Originally, the camp was started in 1974 in the West Campground. The next year, it moved to the Pecan Grove, where Stage 5 is today. After feeling crowded, it later moved to the west end of the Pecan Grove. Stillwater Camp uses "circa 1975" as its start date. The Stillwater Camp mascot was procured in 1990. While on their way to Winfield, some camp members stopped in Newkirk, Oklahoma, at a garage sale and bought a Harmony guitar that they

Button accordionist David Munnelly visits Carp Camp in 2007. The camp attracts some of the world's best musicians and often has an audience that rivals those of the official stages.

were told was fifty years old. They paid one dollar for it. If anyone wandered into their camp without an instrument and wanted to jam with them, they were given the mascot guitar to use.

Located near Stillwater Camp on perhaps the highest point in the Pecan Grove was Gobbler's Knob. Its more than twenty occupants with six camping units had attended for the previous twenty-six years in 2019. The camp's name came from a member who loved to turkey hunt on a farm called "The Knob." Placed out front of the campsite are turkey statues.

The Geezers of Anarchy were celebrating their thirty-fifth anniversary in 2019—or so they thought. The camp was originally known as the "Kansas Acoustic Arts Association." It is located toward the east end of the Pecan Grove and features around twenty-five camping units and about seventy inhabitants.

Camp names and traditions evolve. In 2019, Camp Who was celebrating five years at the festival. Its antecedent was the Biergarten Camp, which was started in 1998. For years, Biergarten hosted a dessert contest. Camp Who became known as a place for Beatles fans.

Camp Sunnyvale, with six years of history, was hosting a French Breton and Celtic music instruction workshop in 2019. Sunnydale was also making plans to combine with ten-year veterans Kamp Keep Me Down to form a new camp called "Lit on the Low Road."

"WINFIELD CHANGED MY LIFE"

There are numerous love and romance stories that have been collected from Winfield over the years, including several campground weddings. The following is the story of Kenny and Rosie Cornell from 2019, when they were attending their twentieth festival together. The story is told in Rosie's own words as they were spoken to *Voice* reporter Ernie Hill:

> *I had been dating my husband a few weeks when, in August 1998, he invited me over for what I thought would be a nice dinner, only to sit me down at the dining room table and say that sentence that strikes fear in every woman's heart, "There is something I need to talk to you about."*
>
> *Expecting the worst, I watched as he opened a shoebox full of pictures. He introduced me to his Winfield friends and proceeded to tell me about a music festival that happened every September in Kansas. He said he wanted*

A parent and child walk through the campground in 2000. Most hours of the day, the campground is quiet and kid friendly.

to invite me but was worried because it could be hard on new couples. I had never heard of bluegrass music, had never attended a music festival, had never heard of Winfield, Kansas, didn't play an instrument or sing and didn't know he was a songwriter who had attended every single Walnut Valley Festival—but I thought it sounded fun. That first year, I went for the last four days and was overwhelmed. I decided to not go back.

The next year, I attended the last four days again, and decided again to not go back. But we were married the next year when September rolled around, so I decided to embrace the festival and make it my own.

Now, twenty years later, I have joined the thousands of people who say, "The Walnut Valley Festival has changed my life." We introduced the festival to our grown children who now camp in Pecan Grove and bring our grandchildren—all of them musicians now. I play the accordion, the guitar and the bass in several old-time and bluegrass bands, write and enter songs in contests (even winning a few) and play on Stage 5 every year. I consider my festival friends among the best I have ever had. I even participated in the pre- and pre-pre–line rushes before Land Rush for the first time this year and plan to do that from now on. I consider myself fortunate to have married a seasoned professional "Winfielder" who showed me the ropes. Without my husband, Kenny Cornell, I would never have heard of Winfield and not been able to say, "Winfield changed my life."

11

HONORED TO MIX

By Greg Smyer

Musician Greg Smyer has been one of the contractors responsible for running sound at Winfield since 1986. Smyer has also appeared on the festival stage with praise and worship band GASS.

Music festival sound has come a long way since Bill Hanley, the "father of festival sound," made his mark in 1969 at the Woodstock Music and Arts Fair. Technology has made it better, but we still live within the constraints of the laws of physics regarding sound.

We are always thinking about what can make sound better for the festival. For sound contractors, traditional "point and shoot" loudspeakers have been replaced by the latest technology of line array loudspeaker systems. The main stages are employing high-end and digital mixing consoles with the latest signal processing and microphone technology. Stages continue to evolve to accommodate musicians for easier access, comfort, lighting and multiple individual monitor mixes.

I have been blessed by the Walnut Valley Association's willingness to invest in acoustic treatment for Stage IV, the contest stage, turning an unintelligible, highly reverberant venue in a metal barn into a decent-sounding venue. These advancements improved a reverb time (RT) of approximately 5.0 seconds to a manageable 1.5 seconds. Similar attention has been devoted to the other three main outdoor stages to provide the best coverage and pattern control.

I believe the first festival during which I ran sound was the event in 1986, the fourteenth Walnut Valley Festival. My music history up to 1986 is a whole other story, but on July Fourth weekends from 1984 to 1986, I helped Kenny Glasgow with sound at Powderhorn Park Bluegrass Festival. I noticed an interesting character in a red jumpsuit who seemed to be observing me mixing and watching the musicians on stage. During a break, I asked Glasgow who the "strange, scary, intimidating" dude was. He just laughed and advised me that it was Bob Redford, the owner and promoter of the WVF.

Shortly before September 1986, Glasgow called me to say that Mr. Redford needed sound for two of the smaller stages (Stage III and Stage IV) at his festival. Glasgow asked if I could run Stage III while he ran Stage IV. I had seen Stage III a few years prior to 1984 and noticed that it only had a small eight-channel mixer and what we called "speakers on sticks." I felt Stage III could benefit from larger-format speakers for better coverage and better sound.

After cutting my teeth on the acoustic music at Powderhorn, I felt confident I could help at Winfield.

I love music. I love mixing sound. As a sound contractor and sound console mixer who is also a musician, I want to provide the best sounding mix that I possibly can. My reward is hearing great music, which, hopefully, I helped bring to people in the audience. As a performing musician, I want the same thing that the artists on stage want—great sound from the person mixing.

As a sound mixer, I am aware that both the festival faithful and Winfield virgins pay their hard-earned money to come that magical third weekend in September, and the last thing they want to hear is bad sound. Finally, as the person at the mixing desk, I know who will be listening to the artists—mothers, fathers, grandparents, wives, husbands, aunts, uncles, cousins, friends—and I know they want their loved one to sound great. Festival organizers and sound contractors take audience feedback seriously, especially in the annual feedback survey form from the festival program. Sometimes, there are things beyond the sound person's control, but most issues can be addressed if they are made known.

I have so many stories I love to share. A few of my more memorable stories include getting "Bob-napped" too many times to mention and John McCutcheon singing for his supper in the old theater barn at Stage III. I remember witnessing the official announcement of the Dixie Chicks by Robin, Laura, Martie and Emily, as they threw out boxes of "Chick-lets" gum to the crowd at Stage III. I cried with the mother of Sara and Sean

Above: The Dixie Chicks play one of their earliest professional shows on Stage III in 1989: (*from left to right*) Martie Erwin Maguire (fiddle), Laura Lynch (guitar), Emily Erwin Strayer (banjo) and Robin Macy (bass). Erwin Maguire had twice finished in the top three of the Walnut Valley Old Time Fiddle Championship. After some lineup changes, the band grew into a country pop powerhouse and won thirteen Grammy Awards. In 2020, the band renamed itself the Chicks.

Right: Harvey Reid plays on Stage III in 1990. Reid was a popular festival act in the late 1980s after winning the National Finger Style Guitar Championship in 1981 and finishing second in the International Autoharp Championship in 1982. Reid, a product of the Washington, D.C. bluegrass scene, helped popularize the use of partial capos and alternate tunings for guitar.

Watkins of Nickel Creek as they performed "The Rose" on Stage III. I was there for the infamous "Don't Tell Bob" set with Spontaneous Combustion—and so was Bob, sitting front and center. I wonder who told him? I saw Tommy Emmanuel's debut on Stage III for a sound workshop. I can still see Linda Tilton's face when she realized I had set up a microphone stand with a work glove on it at her signing position during a John McCutcheon and Tom Chapin show. I loved working with all the incredible musicians, and I enjoyed talking with everyone who has stopped by every year to say hello.

Tim McCulloch kindly offered his advice and knowledge to assist me in making my stages sound better. I will always owe a great debt to Kenny Glasgow for asking me whether I had ever heard bluegrass music and then making sure that I did. I am especially grateful to the WVA for taking a chance on me; Bob and Kendra were literally lifesavers to me. I also appreciate my many festival family members and friends and the incredible musicians I have been honored to mix for.

12

DON'T TELL BOB

By Leo Eilts

Leo Eilts attended Wichita State University. His brother, Roger, went to Bethany College. The brothers have formed the core of several bands, including cowboy band 3 Trails West, winners of the International Western Music Association Duo/Group of the Year Award in 2015. Their "bluerock" band with Scott Prowell and Marvin Gruenbaum was a favorite of the Redford family and WVA audiences.

Spontaneous Combustion first appeared on stage as featured entertainers in 1987. The Walnut Valley Festival poster from that year lists both Spontaneous Combustion and our previous band, the Total Strangers. We were basically the Walnut Valley house band, performing frequently at local churches, public schools, broadcast events, Rotary Club picnics and more campground weddings than I can remember. Basically, we played anywhere Bob Redford wanted us to go.

The jam sessions we hosted at the campsite we called Fort Ridiculous had turned us into a well-established monster late-night jam site. It was common for us to return from a stage show to find a jam already in full swing. Food vendors would bring snacks after closing their concessions to feed the participants. In 1988, Bob Redford surprised us by renaming our campsite "Stage 6," presenting us with an official sign and designating us as an official WVF performance site.

Spontaneous Combustion mug for the camera in 2002: *(from left to right)* Roger Eilts (guitar), Scott Prowell (mandolin), Leo Eilts (bass) and Marvin Gruenbaum (fiddle). The "bluerock" band was the Walnut Valley Association's go-to choice for community and school appearances.

Spontaneous Combustion was on a roll—on the festival bill for eight years straight—so we were surprised to learn that we were not being hired in 1995. Bob's explanation was that while he intended to put us back on the bill in 1996, he wanted to "give us a year off."

But we didn't want to take a year off.

I was in a pout about the prospect of not being on stage that fall when I got a call from Greg Smyer, who is the sound man and de facto manager of Stage III. He said, "What the hell?" And I said, "I know, right?" Stage III had always been our stage of choice, partly because Greg took a personal interest in our band and also because there was virtually no separation between the stage and the audience. So together, we hatched a plan to mount a commando raid, the object being to invade Stage III, if only for a single set, thereby preserving (unofficially) our unbroken string of Walnut Valley appearances.

By the time we arrived in Winfield, the plan was beginning to take shape. The idea was to perform an "after-hours" set and to do so without Bob Redford knowing about it—so we referred to it as the "Don't Tell Bob" show. This plan required that we enlist several hundred coconspirators who were sworn to secrecy.

Before we knew it, Tim Sidebottom was turning out dozens of "Don't Tell Bob" buttons, which were being circulated throughout the campgrounds. I did a short interview on the campground radio with Larry Krudwig, during which I claimed to know nothing of a rumored Spontaneous Combustion show Friday night on Stage III. Larry subsequently made several announcements to the fact that contrary to said rumors, "nothing at all is going to happen on Stage III on Friday at midnight, and if you don't believe it, just go see for yourselves. And don't be late!" Folks were stopping by Stage 6, asking if we were going to perform, to which we replied that we were definitely not playing at midnight on Stage III—and you didn't hear that from us.

It was a bit tricky because there was an unwritten rule, at least at the time, that all stages had to be closed by midnight. There was no doubt that Bob Redford could pull the plug on our plan if he wanted to. Although I never spoke with Bob directly about it, most of the staff were on board and even helping out, so I figured we were good to go. It was turning into one mighty fine prank. It got to the point that you couldn't swing a dead cat anywhere on festival grounds without hitting someone wearing a "Don't Tell Bob" button. Everybody wanted one, and Tim obligingly kept showing up with more buttons every day.

I was in the mobile DJ business at the time and had brought an assortment of DJ toys with me to Winfield. These included a bubble machine, a couple of fog machines, some strobe lights and various other implements. We spent Friday afternoon setting up these items between performances. The entire Stage III crew was in on the plan, and we were absolutely giddy and snickering like schoolboys while preparing for the show.

West Coast band Marley's Ghost played the last official set on Stage III—a set that had belonged to Spontaneous Combustion for years. But when that set was over, Roz Brown, who was the emcee that night, said goodnight to everyone, and the lights went down.

In the dark, we began setting up. We could see that a lot of people were staying in their seats, some even moving forward to get closer to the stage. In the darkness, Roz kept talking to the audience, saying, "Why are you here? There are no shows after midnight. Nothing is happening. There are some good seats down front." Stage I had just closed, and people were walking past Stage III on their way back to the campgrounds, but a lot of them stopped to see what was going on.

When everything was set, still in total darkness, Roz announced "Welcome—whoever this is." The lights came up, and we launched into a song that was a festival favorite at the time, "Dancing in the Moonlight."

I looked into the audience and there, front and center, was the president himself: Bob Redford, grinning like the Cheshire Cat.

13

COMING HOME

By Linda Tilton

Sign artist, clogger and ukulele player Linda Tilton has been a fixture on the Walnut Valley Festival stages for more than thirty years. When Brian Redford died by suicide in 1997, Linda spearheaded a project to honor Brian's memory and contribute to the future of his children.

John McCutcheon said, "We need to bring Linda down to Winfield next year!" And the audience burst into enthusiastic applause. It was 1985, and I was working with John as a sign language interpreter at a concert in Kansas City, Missouri. I had worked with John for a couple of years when he was in the area. John had mentioned me coming to Winfield before. This time, he made sure it happened.

The next year, John brought me to Winfield under the auspices of being his employee to help sell records and tapes after his shows. John was also sure that I'd catch the eye of the festival president. At our first performance at the festival, I was extremely nervous. John has always been generous in helping me prepare by sending me his set list and a recording—back then, a cassette tape—of songs he would perform. But I found the large audience at the Walnut Valley Festival intimidating.

Bob Redford was in the audience, which was creating quite a buzz backstage. While I had never heard of Bob and therefore didn't know the significance of him being there, knowing he was there added to my stress.

After that set, Bob came backstage, shook my hand and introduced himself as the festival owner.

"You're welcome to come to this festival as long as you want," he said. And I've been there every year since.

Being a regular performer at the festival is a joy. I've been a conduit of communication between hearing impaired attendees and stage activities. My presence there has opened people's minds to the idea of the inclusion of individuals who are deaf or hard of hearing to musical events. I've inspired people to learn sign language and even to become interpreters. Most importantly, I was the right person at the right time to help the Redford family in a time of need.

Sign artist Linda Tilton pictured in 2017. First introduced to Walnut Valley Festival organizers by John McCutcheon, Tilton became a fixture on Winfield stages in the 1980s. Tilton brought her whole body into interpreting music, enhancing the experience for both hearing and hard-of-hearing audience members.

In November 1997, tragedy struck the Redford family when Brian, Bob and Kendra's oldest son, died, unexpectedly, leaving behind his wife, Gail, and their children, Kevin and Kayla. Brian loved the festival wholeheartedly and had been an integral part of organizing and running it. His death was a huge blow, not only to Brian's family, but to his Winfield Festival family as well.

As soon as Brian died, the Winfield online discussion group known as the Winfield-l began to discuss how to support the Redford family. A Winfield resident established the "Kevin and Kayla Redford Educational Endowment Fund" at a local bank. The Winfield-l quickly emerged with an idea to create a compact disc and cassette tape as a fundraiser for the endowment fund. Because I had worked with so many entertainers on the stages at Winfield and knew them personally, I became the one to coordinate the project.

And what an amazing project it was. As soon as we decided to go ahead with it, resources seemingly fell out of the sky to make this idea work. The spirit of community collaboration immediately moved into gear. While I had no experience with music production, generous people who did stepped up. The Winfield-l came up with the title *Coming Home: A Winfield Celebration.*

Audience members sign "blue skies," a phrase from "May There Always Be Sunshine," a Russian folk song, in 1989. Musician John McCutcheon led the song in English and Russian, and sign artist Linda Tilton taught fans a sign language version.

They also developed the list of musicians who should be invited to donate one song to the CD. Steve Kaufman sent me a copy of a contract for each musician, songwriter and recording company lawyer, which gave me consent to donate the song's royalties to the education fund.

I set up a post office box and used the Winfield-l to market presales of the album to pay for expenses of the CD's production. As soon as I announced the opportunity to preorder, the orders for CDs and tapes came pouring in.

Each musician sent me a recording of the song they had chosen to donate. Leo Eilts, the bass player with Spontaneous Combustion, donated studio time to organize the songs and created the master that was sent to Oasis, the manufacturer. Stan Rood, from Bluestem, donated the graphic art for the poster, CD cover and booklet. Festival devotee and website designer Don Shorock donated the photographs of each musician. Micah Solomon, the president of Oasis Disc Manufacturing, donated a discount for the CD and tape production.

When I got the delivery of the recordings, Jim Curley, the owner of the Mountain Music Shoppe, organized a packing party and invited a group of people to come to his store to stuff the envelopes that were to be mailed

Todd McGill and Brian Redford set up Stage II's rigging in 1988.

to those who had preordered. Jim also paid for the postage to have them sent out.

At the festival in 1998, I was swamped by people who wanted to buy the album. By Saturday afternoon, it was sold out, and I started taking people's names to preorder a second batch. On Sunday, I contacted Oasis to order a second pressing. They said they had never seen a recording of that size sell out that quickly.

After expenses, approximately $20,000 was added to the endowment fund. The teamwork that was required to create *Coming Home* is a testament to the festival community's huge heart and deep love for the Redford family.

14

FROM GENOVA TO WINFIELD

By Beppe Gambetta

Beppe Gambetta is an acoustic guitar player, composer and music researcher. He has recorded with Charles Sawtelle, Norman Blake, David Grier and Dan Crary. In 2019, the mayor of Genoa named Gambetta "Genoa Ambassador to the World."

September 16, 1992
Winfield, Kansas

Late afternoon, long clouds, sharp fresh wind that comes from distant prairies caressing fields of corn and sunflowers. Everything reminds us that summer is ending, but in Winfield tonight, we warm up with music, food, drinks, fires and, above all, the pleasure of meeting many old music friends after a year. The latest arrivals are setting up their tents. In the air is the smell of burning wood and different foods in preparation (a lot of grilled meat but also a lot of soups and stews) and the sounds of a guitar and banjo in the distance.

Today is Wednesday, and tomorrow, the twenty-first Walnut Valley Festival kicks off in the morning. For such an important event, my friend Haebsi and his wife, Gudrun, decided to fly from Germany and experience this emotion with me, and we will meet tonight at the campsite.

I finally meet Bob Redford, the director of the festival. My friend and colleague Dan Crary told him about me, and he decided to invite me for the

Flat-picker Beppe Gambetta presents a solo set on Stage I in 2018. In twenty Walnut Valley Festival appearances, Gambetta has played his Italian interpretation of American roots music and also introduced the Winfield audience to the forgotten music of the string virtuosi of the early 1900s in Gambetta's native Italy.

first time, happy to add an international touch to his cast of acoustic music excellence. On the bill are Mike Cross, Tom Chapin, John McCutcheon and the "rising stars" Ranch Romance. I will finally be able to hear them, meet them, touch them—and then the big moment will come: Saturday at 5:00 p.m., I will play my first and only set alone on Stage IV, the same stage where the National Flat-Pick Guitar Championship is held.

Bob walks around, extremely busy and dressed in work clothes, welcoming and talking to me like a father, as if music automatically generates a family. He is following the assembly of Stage II in front of a hill, a natural amphitheater, where tomorrow, they will try to beat the Guinness Book of World Records for the largest guitar band in the world. Bob is a tireless worker and personally checks every gear of his machine. He talks to me and in the meantime calls on the "walky-talky," "At Stage II, there are four toilets without toilet paper. Will you take care of this, Krys?" He shows me the festival ground and introduces me to a lot of people; then we move toward the campsite at Russell Brace's Stage 5.

Russell built a new, small stage on a pickup truck for anyone who wants to perform and placed it in the Pecan Grove, the most creative area of the campground. "Get on the list and play your music," Bob tells me. "When they hear you, you'll make lots of new friends." Russell is also very nice. The first available slot is at 2:15 a.m., but it seems that in Winfield, that time is not too late—it is just the beginning of one of the many nights of partying.

Then I find myself alone in the campground with a guitar on my shoulder in search of Haebsi and Gudrun. On the phone, we made a somewhat vague appointment Italian style: "I'll see you on Wednesday evening at the festival campsite." "No problem. We'll look for each other." "Tchüss, see you soon."

But now I discover that the campground at Winfield is quite a large place, sometimes populated by nine thousand people or more, of which at least eight thousand seemingly bring with them an instrument to enjoy the party and experience the music together. I approach the first group of tents and ask, "Sorry, have you heard two German-speaking guys in a tent around here?"

"No, boy, but you have a foreign accent. Where are you from?"

"I'm Beppe, the Italian flat-picker, and I'll play Saturday at 5:00 p.m. at Stage IV."

"Fantastic! Then you have to sit down, taste our fried catfish, have a drink and play something with us."

What a nice welcome. After eating, drinking and playing "Blackberry Blossom," I move, and the scene is repeated shortly after in a small court of RVs. No Germans around, but my new friends have a special amber beer, and the chili con carne has cooked for three hours and is ready. They all play an impeccable "old-time" repertoire, and "Old Joe Clark" becomes our digestif.

This is, of course, just the beginning, with many new encounters for hours and hours, exchanging melodies and toasting until the fingers ache and the head turns. I stop every now and then in the trees to recover, but then I continue my search, fascinated by this place, my wonderland, under colorful drapes, between courts built with hay bales, light installations, kites hanging from trees, food and drink of all kinds, mixed genres, including bluegrass, swing, folk, Celtic—but nowhere can Haebsi and Gudrun be found.

I arrive, exhausted, at 2:15 a.m. at Stage 5 for my short set, and I finally hear Haebsi's voice: "We have been looking for you everywhere. Where have you been?"

Despite the excesses, I manage to perform in some way—I don't know how. But in any case, I get a first hug from that nocturnal audience crowded in front of the truck that became a stage, a stage that welcomes the foreign musician.

Visitors from Switzerland, *(from left to right)* Erwin Beer, Claudio Tolaini, Redford, Ferdinand Zeller, Michael Hunglinger, Kathrin Hunglinger and Antoinetta Vandeventer-Tolaini, in 1987 present WVA president Bob Redford with a cuckoo clock as a token of friendship. Curtis Dick remembered meeting Tolaini at the Wichita airport when picking up artists booked for the festival. That led to several years of Curtis and Sparla hosting music fans from Switzerland in their home during the festival and lifelong friendships. Contest coordinator Karen Deal said Tolaini always brought a case of Swiss chocolate to share on his visits.

But the unforgettable gift will arrive on Saturday. Debuting in a festival with many stages and events of all kinds at the same time is always an unknown. You never know how many people will come to listen to you. In order to not be a complete outsider, I continue devoting my time to people, meeting new friends and joking while in line for corn on the cob, trying out wonderful guitars at the music stands, visiting the Leo and Roger Eilts jam sessions at Stage 6, participating in a guitar workshop with Steve Kaufmann, Dan Crary and Stephen Bennett and dedicating very little time to sleep.

Finally, on Saturday at 4:40 p.m., it is my turn. I'm ready in the backstage area of Stage IV, and I peek at the audience from backstage: "Oh my God! Only seven people!" I decide not to look anymore; I have to concentrate. I just look at the guitar and think only about the program.

Five o'clock comes early, but I hardly notice it. An unforgettable surprise awaits me when I walk on stage: my new friends have come to support me,

Irish trio Socks in the Frying Pan play to a full grandstand in 2016: *(from left to right)* Aodán Coyne (guitar), Shane Hayes (accordion) and Fiachra Hayes (fiddle). In both campground jams and on stages, the festival has celebrated Celtic music over the years. Other performers representing Celtic traditions have included Clanjamfrey, De Dannan, Cherish the Ladies, Eileen Ivers, Colcannon, Connie Dover and David Munnelly.

and all the seats are occupied. Haebsi and Gudrun are smiling on the front row. People are standing at the sides and at the bottom, and the room is packed. Winfield has come to welcome me, and it is the beginning of a love story that has lasted for more than thirty years.

I remember those moments vividly: the emcee who got my name wrong ("From Genova, Italy: Bep Gambada"), to the applause and me starting to play and my standard joke: "I'm the only Italian flat-picker, so I'm the Italian champion! It was quite easy to win!"

15

"MORE A STATE OF MIND THAN A BLUEGRASS FESTIVAL"

By Seth Bate

As the Walnut Valley Festival moved into its teenage years, it was more of an institution than an experiment. The layout, schedule and associated traditions were consistent enough from year to year that returning attendees knew what they could count on. Survey comments such as "It's like we never left once we return" underscored the importance of "coming home to Winfield."

A key to the festival's longevity was its ability to skillfully remain family friendly but also fun for people who wanted to party. The WVA adopted a live-and-let-live attitude that gave campers the freedom to let loose as long as they kept each other safe. Alcohol was tolerated in individual campsites, despite being officially prohibited. Stories of clothing-optional dips in the river circulated widely. Furthermore, a permeable culture was established. The same camper who participated in a tipsy, profane jam circle on Saturday night might join in a gospel sing on Sunday morning.

The commitment to safety and family friendliness was real, as evidenced in advertising, security procedures and in the self-policing by longtime participants. As one fan wrote in a festival survey, "The attendance of all age levels is heartwarming and assures the continuance of bluegrass and indicates the quality of your festival. Your attempts at security have allowed this to happen. Thanks!"

If some in the local community were skeptical about the campfire—and other—smoke in the festival's first years, with time, Winfield embraced the

Special Consensus delivers an animated set on Stage II in 1989: *(from left to right)* Dallas Wayne, Robbie Fulks, Tim Wilson, and Greg Cahill. "Special C" goes back to the 1970s Chicago music scene, and its anchor, banjo player Cahill, teaches at the Old Town School of Folk Music in that city. The band has made ten appearances at Winfield from 1986 to 2019.

event. The city commission declared September 22, 1991, Bob and Kendra Redford Day in recognition of the twentieth festival. This signal of support may have also been a response to rumors that the festival could close or move. While celebrating the anniversary, Bob Redford publicly acknowledged that he had contemplated ending the event that year. "We did not think there was much more we could do creatively, innovatively," he said.

In 1994, Kendra Redford took charge while her husband recovered from surgery. That difficult year led to the Redfords publicly stating that they were looking for ways to become consultants rather than directors, perhaps selling to an internal group of buyers. Bob Redford told a reporter, "We are looking at a change in role as far as leadership or directorship of the festival."

By the festival's twenty-fifth anniversary year, Bob Redford was talking openly to the media about its likely departure. No local offers to purchase the festival had materialized at the time, and the serious offers Redford was considering would move the festival away from Winfield. After a mind-clearing trip to Colorado, Bob Redford resolved to let the operation go after that year's festival.

Before the festival weekend concluded, however, the path changed. "As was quite frequent, Bob changed his mind," Kendra Redford remembered.

Over the years, there have been many efforts to bring festivalgoers from the fairgrounds to other parts of the Winfield community, including golf tournaments, community concerts and a downtown music crawl. In 1988, tours of the Binney and Smith Factory, which manufactured Crayola products, were available.

Roger Wilt shows off a custom-printed National Flat-Picking Contest cooler in 1990. Winfield is the home of the iconic orange Gott cooler. The Gott company was acquired by Rubbermaid in 1986. Rubbermaid and the Walnut Valley Festival collaborated to create a series of products.

Susan Rife, a reporter for the *Wichita Eagle*, covered the Walnut Valley Festival extensively in the late 1980s and early 1990s. The festival has hosted and coordinated media requests and reporters from newspapers, magazines and radio and television outlets from Kansas and around the world.

Saturday night of the silver anniversary festival, festival staff honored the Redfords with souvenir jackets and led them onto the main stage to a huge standing ovation. According to a newspaper account, they conferred between themselves as the audience looked on. "When the applause stopped, [Bob] walked up and said, 'Should I tell them, Kendra?' And she said, 'Bob, you tell them.' He said there would be a '97 festival, and the crowd just lost it again." According to the festival's media release, the decision to continue was made in that moment. The Redfords said they would embark on a slow handoff to their seasoned crew to ensure the festival continued.

A difficult loss for the Redfords after the festival in 1997 cemented the decision to delegate but also introduced an air of uncertainty. The Redfords' son, Brian, had served as the grounds crew chief and director of operations and was in the process of taking over as festival director when he died by suicide.

After Brian Redford's death, Bob Redford began therapy and received a diagnosis that was similar to Brian's—bipolar depression. The Redfords believed that continuing to operate the festival would give Bob a focal point and a reason to work on his mental health, all the while leaning heavily on coordinators and key staff members. In Kendra's assessment, the approach helped both Bob and the festival crew get through the next fourteen years. Deciding what to say about Bob's health, to whom and when was complicated. The Redfords eventually confided in all the WVA staff. "Even though there has been a lot of progress in mental health, there is a lot of stigma there," said Kendra.

The end of the 1990s brought the death of one of the festival's founders. Though his association with the Walnut Valley Festival was only one of Stuart Mossman's adventures, the "guitar maker, dreamer and entrepreneur" was remembered as one of the small handful of people who got the festival rolling. In 2010, recognizing Mossman as a pivotal figure in the evolution of guitar building, director Barry Brown released the documentary *Stuart Mossman: A Modern Stradivari*, which depicted Mossman's long relationship with the Carradine brothers, David, Keith and Bobby.

Bluegrass Event of the Year

Meanwhile, the Walnut Valley Festival achieved official international recognition. The International Bluegrass Music Association nominated WVF for "Bluegrass Event of the Year." Bob Redford traveled to the IBMA Convention to give a presentation about marketing bluegrass festivals and attend the awards ceremony; to his surprise, the envelope revealed that WVF was the winner. Though the Winfield festival rarely presented the top echelon of touring bluegrass acts, it was recognized for its commitment to booking up-and-coming players. Not surprisingly, the IBMA selection committee also was influenced by the festival's organization and by the sense of community and level of musicianship among its campground and parking lot pickers. "It's more a state of mind than just a bluegrass festival," said an IBMA spokesperson.

More recognition followed as the festival entered its fourth decade. In 2012, Bob Redford was honored by *Ingram's* magazine as one of the "Fifty Kansans You Should Know." Redford's legacy as an entrepreneur was recognized the same year by Southwestern College with its Business Builder Award. These moments of recognition had an air of marking a transition.

Indeed, the owners continued to praise, empower and depend on their crew chiefs and key staff members. Some crew chiefs described the handoff

IBMA
International Bluegrass Music Association

September 15, 1999

Bob Redford
Walnut Valley Festival
PO Box 245
Winfield, KS 67156

Dear Mr. Redford,

On behalf of the International Bluegrass Music Association, I would like to let you know that the Walnut Valley Festival is one of the finalists for the first IBMA award for Bluegrass Event of the Year.

The other two finalists are the Grass Valley Bluegrass Festival in Grass Valley, California, and the Bill Monroe Bean Blossom Bluegrass Festival in Bean Blossom, Indiana.

The finalists will be recognized and the winner will be announced for this award at the Special Awards Luncheon on Thursday, October 21, from noon - 2 p.m. (EST), at the Galt House in Louisville, Ky., as a part of the IBMA Trade Show.

We are planning a multi-media slide and audio presentation as a part of the Special Awards Luncheon. At your earliest convenience please send two or three photos or slides of the festival, to the IBMA office. We also need to play some music in the background when your festival is being announced and the slides are being shown. Do you have a preference of which artist we play - perhaps a group who has performed at your festival recently? Please send the photos or slide, along with your ideas for a musical background, to Nancy Cardwell, IBMA, 207 E. Second Street, Owensboro, KY 42303.

I hope that you will be able to be with us at the Special Awards Luncheon. You may already be registered for the IBMA Trade Show. If not, please give me a call and I'll fill out the forms to comp your Trade Show registration for Thursday, Oct. 21. If you will not be able to attend the Trade Show this year, please let me know who will accept the trophy for you in the event that you win the award.

Congratulations, and thanks for hosting such a great event in Winfield to showcase bluegrass music.

Sincerely,

Nancy Cardwell
IBMA Special Projects Coordinator
888-GET-IBMA

BOARD OF DIRECTORS

OFFICERS

STAFF

207 East Second Street
Owensboro, Kentucky
42303 USA

A letter to Bob Redford, the trophy and the award logo on a crew T-shirt commemorate the Walnut Valley Festival winning the Bluegrass Event of the Year Award from the International Bluegrass Music Association in 1999. Redford and Rex Flottman traveled to Louisville, Kentucky, for the ceremony.

process as two steps forward and one step back as Bob Redford wavered between letting go and hanging on.

Having an experienced and nimble crew proved to be critical in 2008. Many previous years had been rainy or muddy, and in 1973, the festival had narrowly missed being flooded out. Other years, festival workers pitched in with City of Winfield personnel to clean up and rebuild after weather emergencies to keep the fairgrounds in good shape all year round.

In 2008, after most of the year's set up work had been completed, the Walnut River rose over the campground. The stage shows and crafts went on more or less as usual, but a community of thousands of campers was displaced. As Bob Hamrick wrote, "A fleet of tractors showed up with log chains, pulling everything from VW buses to castle-sized RVs out of the rising tide."

Most campground traditions continued at Winfield City Lake and other nearby camping spots, and some new ones were launched, but the year was hard on festival revenue. A similar situation occurred eight years later. While experience and communication technology made the second flood

Right: Sierra Hull leads her band in 2010 on Stage II. Hull went on to be the International Bluegrass Music Association Mandolin Player of the Year four times, most recently in 2021.

Below: Jerry O'Neil and his Kubota tractor extricate a camper from the mud in 2008. While the 2008 flood was particularly dramatic, closing the campgrounds after early arrivers had already set up, similar rescues have taken place many times over the years. In particular, campers who have chosen low spots frequently need help when trying to depart on Sunday. "Strangers with tractors" are a welcome sight to those stuck in the mud.

experience smoother, it still required crews to effectively set up and tear down for the event twice. And again, it affected revenues.

If technology was a help during the 2016 flood, it was a mixed blessing for the WVA in the second half of the festival's existence. The proliferation of the World Wide Web and email listservs in the 1990s and early 2000s made it easier to compile and share information from the staff to the rest of the world, and it helped campground communities cement their identities and plan for their festival experiences. A Yahoo-based listserv created its own meetups, events and T-shirts. Don Shorock, an obsessive music enthusiast from Great Bend, Kansas, created elaborate online documentation of the festival. In 2006, a Facebook group eventually known as the Walnut Valley Bluegrass Festival Fans began; it grew to have more than eleven thousand members. The speed of communication, however, also meant that rumors, complaints and misunderstandings were shared widely among WVF fans—sometimes to the consternation of staff.

Festival staff always arranged stages with an eye to the way photographs would look. As technology changed and nearly every festivalgoer had a phone with a camera, this awareness grew more acute. Video recording was more problematic. While staff made little effort over the years to control audio recordings of concerts, video was prohibited, and stage crews were expected to monitor the audience for evidence of video recording. This grew harder as technology improved. Starting around 2016, the WVA barred unauthorized drones from the festival out of concern for crowd safety should a drone fall into a crowd or strike a power line or stage rigging.

With the fiftieth anniversary of the festival in sight, new efforts to document the annual homecoming began. The Cowley County Historical Museum established a permanent exhibit for the festival. Assisted by art director Bryan Masters, writer Bob Hamrick produced *September's Song*, a coffee table book that collected various elements of the Winfield experience through stories, quotes and innumerable photographs. When a neighboring store closed, the WVA office on Winfield's Main Street took over the space and began the process of making it a retail space and place to display festival artifacts.

For the first time, however, the WVA was proceeding without guidance from one of its three festival founders. Bob Redford died on December 17, 2016. News of his passing was shared in bluegrass publications and on websites, Wichita's television news programs and KFDI radio, among other media. At the festival in 2017, stage crews enlarged a poignant cartoon expressing appreciation for Redford and set it by the main stage. Richard

John McCutcheon on Stage I in 2017. Cartoonist and banjo player Richard Crowson acknowledged the passing of Bob Redford in one of his annual Walnut Valley–themed cartoons. Festival organizers used the image as part of the Stage I decoration.

Richard Crowson captures the Winfield spirit of passing the music on in a cartoon published in 2003. Crowson created a series of cartoons about the Walnut Valley Festival, often contrasting the festival's relaxed atmosphere with tense current events. In 2003, the Recording Industry Association of America was pursuing lawsuits against several websites where copyrighted musical recordings were exchanged. *Courtesy of Richard Crowson.*

Crowson, a banjo player and contributor to the *Wichita Eagle* and KMUW radio, created the drawing.

Is the Walnut Valley Festival timebound to one generation—or to one set of individuals?

The WVA and the Redford family are testing that question. A handoff that had been haltingly attempted in past years began in earnest in early 2018. Festival owner Kendra Redford announced that her son Bart would assume the role of executive director and take responsibility for organizing the festival. "I feel very lucky to be able to come home to WVA and to work in an organization that for me feels more like a family than a business. That's understandable, given that every member of my family has worked at WVA at some point," said Bart Redford.

Winfield 48.5

Commitment to the Walnut Valley experience appeared strong, at least among the current festival fans, even after Redford's passing. The certainty of the festival each year, with its traditions and reassuring sameness, provides solace in an uncertain age. As writer Bill Graham put it, "Loyal festivalgoers swear that they'll show up at the Cowley County Fairgrounds in Winfield on the third weekend in September whether there's an organized festival or not.…The campground mantra is 'forty more years.'"

That commitment was seriously tested for the first time in 2020. A global pandemic of the novel coronavirus did what Kansas weather never could. The in-person festival was canceled.

"Winfield 48.5" was billed as a virtual festival. It included live online workshops and streamed concerts, most of them prerecorded. The event brought about the return of a battle of the bands competition, now handled through online voting, and led to an effort the following year to provide a livestream from in-person festival stages. Despite the promise of these innovations and the goodwill generated among artists and audience members, Bart Redford admitted that he hoped a virtual festival is never again necessary.

In 2021, the Winfield stages were again live. Some schedule shuffling was required, and staffing was a challenge for organizers, but the event took place with no significant mishaps. It was the debut of an online process to streamline "Land Rush," the race to preferred campsites. The festival's

A masked couple peruses crafts in 2021. With infection rates down and weather hot, the Walnut Valley Association held its forty-ninth festival a year later than planned. Health officials offered onsite COVID vaccinations, and face coverings and hand sanitizer were available throughout the festival grounds.

The Walnut Valley Festival has been (mostly) kid friendly from its inception—even on stage. Lily and Abigail Chapin hold babies on Stage I in 2016 while performing with Tom Chapin and friends, including the band Steel Wheels, bass player Michael Mark and keyboard player Jon Cobert.

alcohol policy was changed to bring it in line with the reality on the ground, and for the first time, organizers experimented with a beer and wine garden featuring local brews inside the interior area. Organizers also marked the longtime dedication—and recent flexibility—of staff members and previewed fiftieth anniversary festival plans with a ceremony on Stage I. And on Stage III, a mix of campground singers and stage artists debuted a set of songs planned for *Winfield, A Bluegrass Musical.*

The Walnut Valley Festival is a unique institution with its own character, culture and traditions. Trent Wagler graduated from high school in Kansas and now performs at festivals, including WVF, with his band, the Steel Wheels. He also helps run the band's own festival, Red Wing Roots, in Virginia. Wagler said fondly that the WVF "feels like a festival created by people who had never been to one. One of the refreshing things about Winfield is that it's very successful at just doing what it does and being who it is."

16

REFLECTIONS ON FIFTY YEARS

By Orin Friesen

Radio personality and musician Orin Friesen is the author of Goat Glands to Ranch Hands: The KFDI Story *and* Honky-Tonkers & Western Swingers: Stories of Country Music in Wichita, Kansas.

As I look back over fifty years of Walnut Valley Festivals, I'm flooded with memories. Perhaps I shouldn't have used the word "flood," as we've had to deal with flood issues more than once at Winfield. It seems like the weather always wants to play a role in festival events. I've attended the festival wearing a T-shirt or a warm coat, sometimes on the same weekend. However, my memory has taken the rough edges off the weather issues. I mostly remember pleasant, late summer days and the advent of WVF letting me know that we're heading into autumn.

Though I usually venture into the campgrounds several times during the festival, my personal perspective of what I refer to as "Winfield" is centered on the main stages. It started out at the very first festival, when my band was offered a guest slot during an open time between scheduled performers. I could point out that this was on Stage I. But then again, there was only one stage.

I have performed on the Winfield stages as a member of six or seven bands over the years and have been a stage emcee for most of the fifty years. My personal collection of recorded music contains hundreds and hundreds of LPs and CDs by artists I first saw perform at Winfield: New Grass Revival,

Jack and Mike Theobald and the Bluegrass Country Boys play their Kansas version of bluegrass in 1974. This lineup of the band, later known simply as Bluegrass Country, is Fred Morton (fiddle), Mike Theobald (banjo), Orin Friesen (mandolin), Jack Theobald (guitar) and Dan Kocks (bass). Jack Theobald founded the first bluegrass band in the state, and the Theobalds were likely the first to air bluegrass music on Kansas radio. Friesen began his own weekly bluegrass radio show in 1973.

Wichita-area "moo-grass" band Home Rangers play Stage III in 1997: *(from left to right)* Richard Crowson (dobro), Stan Greer (guitar), Orin Friesen (bass) and David Hawkins (mandolin). Humor is a key ingredient in Western music, and the Home Rangers brought it front and center. Friesen has perhaps logged more stage time at Winfield than anyone else. He has appeared with multiple bands, including the Home Rangers, the Prairie Rose Wranglers and the Prairie Rose Rangers, and has served as an emcee.

Hot Rize (*from left to right*): Pete Wernick, Tim O'Brien, Nick Forster and Charles Sawtelle in 1981, as the band was starting to climb from a Boulder, Colorado–based act to a national bluegrass sensation. The band chose the name Hot Rize as a nod to a longtime sponsor of bluegrass music, Martha White Flour.

Hot Rize, J.D. Crowe with Tony Rice, Country Gazette, Alison Krauss, the Dixie Chicks, Beppe Gambetta, Claire Lynch, Lester Flatt, Dan Crary, Tom Chapin, Tom Paxton, Byron Berline, John McCutcheon, Bryan Bowers, Don Reno, Mike Cross, Norman Blake and countless others.

My life would be completely different had I not started going to Winfield in 1972. That Winfield fever has spread to my family. My kids grew up attending the festival and have made it a part of their annual routine. Every January, when we start planning for the new year, the first thing we do is block out the third weekend of September. The festival dates are automatic holidays for us, just like Christmas, Easter and the Fourth of July. Our family motto can be seen on the blue-and-yellow Walnut Valley Festival stickers, "I can't. I'm going to Winfield!"

I spend most of my time at the festival in places that most folks never get to go—behind the scenes. Life backstage at Winfield is almost like having a family reunion every hour. The other emcees and stage managers become like my immediate family, and as each group of performers arrive, usually more than an hour before their scheduled show, it's like the arrival of cousins you haven't seen in years. There are hugs all around, followed by "How've you been?" or "What have you been up to?" Before long, the

Art Thieme and Mike Cross appreciate one another's antics on stage in 1982. Thieme, a one-time manager of the Chicago School of Folk Music, and Cross, who grew up steeped in Appalachian traditions, shared a love of wordplay and humorous stories. Thieme appeared at the June Jamboree and ten Walnut Valley Festivals before retiring from performing for health reasons in the 1990s. Cross was on the bill sixteen times.

From left to right: Mark O'Connor, Dan Crary, Tony Rice and Dudley Murphy lead a flat-pick workshop in 1983.

Longtime festival emcees Mike Shirkey (*left*) and Mike Flynn (*right*) compare notes backstage in 1991. The Walnut Valley Festival has selected emcees and stage managers carefully, often tapping people with experience in broadcasting or presenting concerts. Shirkey hosts public radio's "The Pickin' Post" and its associated concert series in Arkansas. Flynn hosts the syndicated radio show "The Folk Sampler."

entertainers take their instruments from their cases and begin tuning them, then head into the warm-up area to figure out their set list or brush up on a few songs.

Mealtime for the performers is another special time when we gather at John and Becky Conway's chuckwagon behind Stage I. Sitting at the picnic tables beside the chuckwagon has the feel of a small-town church picnic, with entertainers, emcees, stagehands and other festival workers all mixed together, sharing great food and friendly conversation. For many years, the highlight of those chuckwagon gatherings was when festival owner Bob Redford would drop by for a visit. Everyone enjoyed seeing Bob and having a bit (or a lot) of conversation with him.

Backstage at Winfield is one of my "happy places," but it can also be a sad place, especially as the festival draws to a close each year. I often work Stage I on Sunday afternoon. As I stand backstage, I notice a continuing stream of campers leaving the fairgrounds. Even though I may be starting to get tired, I'm wishing those campers would all stay a while longer because I don't want the festival to end. It's also bittersweet when entertainers drop by to say goodbye as they head out for their next event somewhere down the road. As I get that final hug or handshake, I wonder if we'll meet here again next September or years later?

After having been at Winfield for fifty years, I have come to realize that a friendly farewell might be the last personal contact I may ever have with that person. I've learned to cherish those moments. But come hell or high water, I'm always ready to be back again the next year.

17

WINFIELD OVER TIME

By John McCutcheon

John McCutcheon may be the performer most associated with the Walnut Valley Festival. He is a groundbreaking hammer dulcimer player, Woody Guthrie scholar, prolific songwriter, storyteller and enthusiastic leader of group singing. He is the author of Happy Adoption Day! *and* Christmas in the Trenches, *both adapted from his songs.*

In the spring of 1979, my phone rang. A fellow named Art Coats introduced himself as an organizer from a festival in Kansas. He said he'd heard my first couple of albums and thought I might be a good fit. He asked if I would come.

Although I was a solo performer, I had recently begun playing with a couple of neighbors in southwest Virginia, two guys with whom I shared a love of both the breadth and depth of Appalachian music. Impulsively, I blurted, "How 'bout I come as part of a trio?"

"Sure," he responded, without asking for so much as a demo.

Upon revealing this surprise gig to one of my new "bandmates," he drolly said, "We've never been to Kansas."

About two weeks before we were to drive halfway across the country, one the fellows broke his wrist. I assumed we'd have to cancel.

"Nah," Art said when I called with the news, "Come as a duo, we'll work something out."

And that's how my relationship with Winfield began. I showed up with two-thirds of the planned band and no duo repertoire. We did, indeed, "work something out." I grabbed another fiddle player from here, a guitarist from there, snagged a bass player—and we put on a show that everyone knew we were producing entirely from our posteriors. And they loved it. Go figure.

John McCutcheon closes a set, inviting the audience to sing along, in 2012. The multi-instrumentalist, songwriter, storyteller and world traveler has been a staple of the Walnut Valley Festival and a participant in—or instigator of—many of its innovations, including the virtual festival that was held in 2020. McCutcheon's album of songs written for the festival is called *Welcome the Traveler Home: The Winfield Songs*.

So from the beginning, I knew that Winfield was not merely about one concert after another. It was about seeing something unexpected, something festive. It was about dancing on the wire.

In a trade in which musicians are everyone else's spare time, in which we work evenings and weekends, in which we have to leave our homes and our families to earn a living, it's a rare and welcome thing to feel like you're coming home. But that is Winfield.

"Coming home" to Winfield is easy and it makes my job more fun. I don't have to devote time introducing myself to an audience that doesn't know me. I can get right down to work. Winfield is as comfortable as an old pair of boots.

Our festival is home to every possible acoustic instrument contest. And despite the fact that I have a reputation of knowing my way around all those instruments, I discovered early on that that is not what the crowd expects or wants from me. Sure, I'll rear back and play something mildly impressive on the hammer dulcimer or the banjo (even the didgeridoo a time or two) but the songs, the stories, are what people want—and that chance to join their voices and sometimes their hands in unison. It is one thing to sit in the grandstands with thousands of other people and watch a show. It is another thing entirely to dare to join in, to risk harmony, to be in awe at what's being created among a crowd of strangers. It is a transcendent thing to be a part of that, and believe me, it is felt on stage.

It is that sense of community at Winfield that somehow refuses to allow its musicians to be stars. To get from Stage I to Stage III, you have to walk right down the midway, the Main Street of the festival. Inevitably, people will stop you but not for an autograph—usually just for a chat. I've never once been made to feel awkward or put upon. It's usually a story or a thank-you or a "here's the baby we just had." That said, most folks simply leave you alone and let you enjoy a part of the festival you'll never see from backstage.

As I look back on my many years with the festival, a number of unforgettable moments come to mind.

The conversation I had after a Stage II show in which a middle-aged man said, "I proposed to my wife after one of your sets!" A young teenage girl, standing nearby and not to be outdone, offered, "I was conceived after one of your sets!" Boy, I wish I could remember that set.

There was the Saturday night I invited Bob Franke, songwriter of "The Great Storm Is Over," up on the main stage to help me with that song. I'll never forget the look on his face as five thousand people reintroduced him to the song they'd adopted by singing and signing it back to him.

There was also the Friday night Tommy Emmanuel and I were lost in an impromptu jam backstage with some banjo-guitar pyrotechnics when I heard myself being introduced. I turned to him and said, "Hey, come on up and let's play this for my opening song." During the post-song ovation, he

The Winfield Regional Symphony gets a standing ovation at the end of its Stage I performance in 1994. The symphony orchestra, conducted by Gary Gackstatter, appeared as the backing band for John McCutcheon and Tom Chapin.

The audience at Stage II stands in a moment of reflection in 2001, days after a terrorist attack rocked the nation. Performers and audience members responded together in a number of ways throughout the weekend, including moments of silence, musical tributes and coordinated singalongs.

leaned in and grinned, "OK, mate, what's next?" He did the entire show with me, improvising some of the tastiest, most understated guitar parts I've ever heard. I was as entranced as the audience.

There is another Winfield, one that might be easily missed by those attending. In 1996, the festival asked Tom Chapin and me to perform with the Winfield Regional Symphony. It was to be a featured concert on Sunday afternoon. But to accommodate the symphony, they would need to greatly expand the acreage of Stage I, and that work fell to the festival crew. As soon as the final notes of the Saturday night concert faded away, they mobilized. Forklifts, hand carts, carpenters and dozens of volunteers sprang into action. These generous people worked quite literally through the night to transform the stage. They finished moments before the 11:00

a.m. rehearsal. This feat is emblematic of the dedication and hard work that makes the festival possible.

Of all my recollections, the most poignant was the twenty-two-hour drive my trusty road manager Tommy and I made after a canceled flight just two days after 9/11. When I catatonically took the stage, it must have been God who told me to play "This Land Is Your Land." And the entire audience, my sweet Winfield family, helped one another up, joined hands and sang that song of defiance, of inclusion, of the best kind of patriotism. I wasn't surprised. It was Winfield. I was home.

CONCLUSION

By Bart Redford

I am writing this in March 2021 and am now cautiously optimistic that we will be able to have our forty-ninth Walnut Valley Festival at the Winfield fairgrounds in September. We see some promising signs in terms of the overall trend of new COVID-19 cases, the tempo of vaccinations, as well as the announcements being made by other venues and festivals. I am attempting to pause and reflect, to see what lessons we might learn from this year.

In the office, we began 2020 much like any other year, looking forward to a gradual but steady uptick in our workload as we advanced toward September. Most of the entertainers had been hired, the poster was almost finished and we were talking with concessions and craftspeople about the coming year.

As COVID-19 spread gradually around the globe from January to March, we began to realize how difficult it would be to hold a festival in 2020. While in late March Kansas still seemed to be much better off than many states, outbreaks on the East and West Coasts advanced steadily inward, and we began to see more and more notices of cancellations or postponements of major festivals. Events dropped off schedules one by one.

Like most businesses, WVA initially implemented a work-from-home regime. After some modifications were made, though, most staff opted to return to the office, keeping mostly to our individual offices and maintaining masks and social distancing in the common areas. WVA leadership met repeatedly as we reviewed various scenarios and different options. Using the information available to us, we tried to predict whether COVID-19 cases might decline over the summer.

They did not, of course, and in fact, the infection rate climbed higher than we had ever feared it might. Even now, it is difficult to fathom that more than five hundred thousand Americans have died from the virus to date.

We decided in early June to postpone WVF 49 to 2021. Instead of gathering on the Walnut River in September, we declared we would hold a virtual festival, dubbed WVF 48.5, to tide us through until next year. We had benefited from seeing many festivals that had already crossed this bridge, and we spent quite a few weekends watching how others navigated this challenge.

Importantly, before we went public with our announcement, we reached out to every performer and most of our vendors and craftspeople, letting them know what was coming. You cannot imagine how touching it was to reach out to artists and agents, most of whom had been receiving these cancellation calls for months already, and have them ask if there was anything they could do to support us—to support Winfield.

While preparing for a virtual festival, we were faced with a bewildering array of questions that needed to be answered and quickly. Live or prerecorded concerts? Which platform to use? Free streaming with a chance to donate or pay-per-view? What are the best times of the day for streaming? One would think that dispensing with the need to prepare the grounds, to set up stages, fencing and all the other requirements of a live festival, would make things so much easier. But for us, it was very much a step into the great unknown.

Luckily, we had an entrepreneurial staff, and we had help from so many people (including managers of other festivals) who shared their expertise with us. We would have been sunk without the assistance of our longtime videographers, Legleiter Video Productions, and our website designers, Custom Internet Services. I also want to thank the staff of the Legacy Community Foundation and Winfield Arts and Humanities Council, who provided support for our fundraising efforts.

I should also note that during this difficult time, we received Payment Protection Plan support and a Shuttered Venue Operators Grant from the federal government and a Small Business Working Capital Grant from the State of Kansas. Without that support, we would have been forced to shut down the office entirely and furlough our staff for a significant part of the year. Whatever your political stance, I hope you understand that these

Festival emcees Andrea Springer (*left*) and Orin Friesen (*right*) record video introductions for the virtual WVF in 2020. The COVID-19 pandemic forced the cancellation of the in-person festival for the first time, something weather had never done. Festival organizers created WVF 48.5, which included free online concerts, a virtual battle of the bands and virtual workshops on Zoom.

programs kept a lot of people employed in similar businesses and out of the unemployment line. We were very grateful for the help.

When we started work on a virtual festival, we did so with the intent of generating much-needed revenue for both artists and us. But we also knew that people wanted and needed some uplift in a time when many were feeling isolated and missing that annual gathering down by the Walnut River. We debated making the event one that required the purchase of a ticket, but I'm glad that we ultimately went with a concept that allowed anyone to access the streaming videos and rewarded donors with some choice souvenirs.

To those who contributed to WVF 48.5 over the course of that week, I want to thank you from the bottom of my heart. Your contributions benefited not only the artists who took part but helped keep WVF 49 on track as well. We heard from many people who had not been able to make it to Winfield in some time, telling us how much they enjoyed being able to watch their favorite performers once again, if only online. We also heard from people who had elderly parents or other loved ones who were able to tune in and who appreciated the free access to the programming. The gifts we offered to financial supporters took longer than we anticipated to create and deliver, but we hope they were worth the wait.

As much as I look forward to a day when we can meet down at the fairgrounds without masks and without having to forgo the traditional "welcome home" hugs from campmates upon arrival, we did make some discoveries in 2020. No one likes being forced to change, but I think we can all agree that sometimes those changes can bring unexpected benefits—some we intend to maintain or repeat if we can.

First, the modern re-creation of the battle of the bands was one of the highlights of WVF 48.5. We had some serious contenders in terms of the bands that entered, and it was a close-run race right until the end of the voting. Pretend Friend, a band that was well known in the campgrounds, won the right to be hired as part of our official lineup for WVF 49 in 2021.

The inspiration for this contest emerged from this very book project. I was looking through some old WVF programs and, for the first time, really noticed the bluegrass band contest that had been organized in the early years of the festival. (In my defense, I was only six years old at the time of our first WVF.) It seemed like something that we could easily adapt for an online event, and I was happy to see that it really took off.

In fact, I've seen some other festivals that are now doing something similar. We have some tweaking to do, but we intend to hold virtual band contests early enough to have the bands included in our roster for subsequent festivals. We think it is a great way to capitalize on the talent of our local and regional bands, the ones you see so often in the campgrounds, and bring them to a larger audience on the official stages.

I think our NewSong Showcase also showed us the benefits of organizing some online elements for this proud tradition at Winfield. We love giving a stage to the songwriters selected every year for this honor, but providing videos online from the artists does have some advantages. For one thing—and we heard this repeatedly from the participants—it allows the songwriter to do multiple takes (if necessary) to get it just right. Some even included outtakes in their video submission, which were great fun. This approach also gives us the chance to showcase their talents beyond the stages here in Winfield.

We are not sure how we are going to accomplish this, but it is on our minds to reach out to our legion of songwriter supporters in camps at Winfield and see if we can find a way to extend the virtual elements of the showcase in coming years.

The online workshops were also quite popular, although I think folks got a little burned out on the idea as more and more offerings came online over the course of the year. Still, I think that talented artists were able to make a transition to online teaching, and that means that many music students have access who would never have had the chance before 2020. That is especially important for those of us who live in towns where there aren't many folks who teach the banjo or mountain dulcimer, just as examples. I'm not honestly sure how this will fly in years when we are able to have the live workshops, but we will explore it.

Finally, all the nice comments we received from people who were able to share their virtual Winfield with folks who have never been here or folks who are just not able to attend for one reason or another have convinced us to explore the possibility of offering a live feed from one of our stages. We have been doing this on a limited basis for a few portions of the festival already. In 2019, we livestreamed our entire Champions Concert, the evening devoted to watching last year's contest winners come back and show us what they can do when they aren't constrained by contest rules. The nice thing about that was seeing the champions' family members and friends back home watching and commenting online. There are some technical and legal challenges involved in our streaming the entire program of one stage, but I can tell you that it is something we are looking at very closely.

There were also a few elements of WVF 48.5 that had originally been intended to be part of our fiftieth celebration. A Walnut Valley Land Rush Game was something that we were already working on, and we have quite a few more copies that we will be selling at WVF 49 and 50 (and beyond, most likely). We also got a little more time—thankfully—to put together this book project, and I would like to think the extra time has resulted in a superior product. If you agree, let Seth Bate know, because he has managed this project from start to end.

We have some other tricks up our sleeves, some things that we intend to do in our fiftieth year. And they include an entire musical devoted to the magic of Winfield. It is titled, appropriately enough, *Winfield, a Bluegrass Musical.* The production was written by Kenneth Gale, who completed it over the summer of 2020. While some of us were sitting around during the pandemic catching up on Netflix, Ken wrote a funny musical with some quite memorable numbers, all about a magical place we like to call our pickers paradise. It is about a boy and a girl, a songwriting contest and a guitar or two; it involves several campsites, and there is even a song devoted to Stella. Ken plays a number of instruments himself. Ken and his wife, Karen, have been conducting in-depth field research in the campgrounds for the last few years.

An enthusiastic group of musicians debut the songs from Ken Gale's forthcoming production *Winfield, A Bluegrass Musical*: (*from left to right*) Luke Haaksma (hammer dulcimer), Jim Winters, Joseph Ranaghan (fiddle), Gale, Roger Eilts, Emily Johnson-Erday (banjo), Leo Eilts, Helen Avakian, David Irwin, Corey Johnson-Erday (guitar) and Jim Herrmann (bass). Not pictured is Bing Futch. Winters, Eilts and Eilts make up 3 Trails West. Avakian and Irwin perform together as Red Door Duo. *Seth Bate.*

While I try to focus on things that can be learned from 2020, I know that I will always see it as a year of loss. I know that there is the direct cost in terms of the lives lost and the people who will be suffering the effects from COVID-19 for a long time. But there were also so many plans made that were never realized, events that didn't happen, all the businesses that opened and closed immediately for lack of patronage. And for live music, it was a year that put many venues, artists, agents and promoters out of business. We have not yet seen the full effects of this, and I am sure we are going to see ramifications of this pandemic echo for many years to come.

I think one of the long-term effects is likely a further erosion in our collective sense of community. In 1995, Robert Putnam chronicled the reduction in America of all forms of in-person social interaction in an essay, "Bowling Alone: America's Declining Social Capital," later an influential book. If the practice of bowling alone in the late twentieth

Top: The Prairie Acre jams on the midway at sunset in 2009. *From left to right*: Noah Musser (banjo), Greg Yother (guitar), Tricia Spencer (fiddle, carrying Ruby Yother) and Virginia Musser (bass, carrying Kellar Musser). Virginia Musser said, "We hauled those kids everywhere on our backs—Stage 7, Stage 5 and all over the campgrounds....My kids hadn't missed a single Winfield until the pandemic."

Bottom: Stage II, set at the base of a hill that rises to the south, creates a natural amphitheater of sorts. Its audience filled the hill in 1987.

century was symptomatic of a gradual decline of our sense of community, then I think that the 2020 pandemic was probably equivalent to dropping social connection off a cliff.

I generally try to be realistic about what we do here. We run a music festival. We aren't working on the cure for cancer, we aren't producing the next ground-breaking technology that will revolutionize the workplace and it is unlikely we are going to achieve world peace, you and me. But I think the reason folks come back to Winfield year after year has less to do with our lineup, the crafts or the contests—as amazing as they all may be—and more to do with that sense of community that they feel when we are here. People express that in many different ways. "It's like coming home." "It's like Christmas in September." Or as contributor Ginger Thomas put it in the *WVA Voice* one year, "It's like *Cheers*, where everybody knows your name." I don't think it is any accident that those are expressions about how we feel when we are here.

And I think that if ever we are in need of reactivating that sense of connection to each other, it must be in this post-pandemic world. I hope that Winfield will continue to do that for you and for many others in the years to come.

Appendix A
Walnut Valley Festival Milestones

By Bart Redford and the WVA Staff

1972

The first festival was called Walnut Valley Bluegrass Festival and National Flat-Picking Championship.

There were two contests: National Flat-Picking Championship and Bluegrass Band.

1973

A crafts fair was added.

A bluegrass fiddle contest was added.

1974

The festival was then called the National Guitar Flat-Picking Championship Bluegrass Music and Folk Arts and Crafts Festival.

A banjo contest was added.

1976

An additional festival was held in the spring, the Walnut Valley Spring Thing.

Two new contests were added at the Spring Thing, the National Tut Taylor Dobro Championship and the Mountain Dulcimer.

There was a final bluegrass band contest.

1977

The festival was then called the National Flat-Picking Championship Folk Arts and Crafts Festival.

The National Hammer Dulcimer and Walnut Valley Mandolin Contests were added.

1979

The festival was then called the National Flat-Picking Championship Acoustic Music Folk Arts-Crafts Festival.

An additional festival was held in the summer, the June Jamboree.

1980

In its ninth year, the festival was billed as the Walnut Valley Festival.

There were seven contests: the National Finger-Pick Guitar Championship, the National Flat-Pick Guitar Championship, the National Mountain Dulcimer, the National Hammer Dulcimer, the National Bluegrass Banjo, the Walnut Valley Old-Time Fiddle and the Walnut Valley Mandolin Contests.

1981

The International Autoharp Contest was added to make eight total contests.

The Feisty logo debuted.

1984

The WVA moved into an office of its own at 918 Main Street.

1987

The WVA sponsored a two-day event at the Starlight Theatre in Kansas City.

Stage Five made its first appearance in the Pecan Grove.

1989

Stage Six made its first appearance in the West Campground.

Muriel Anderson became the first female National Finger Style Champion.

1991

This was Andy May's first Acoustic Kids Showcase at Winfield.

There was a world record largest guitar band attempt (572 members) and a world record largest acoustic band attempt (770 members).

1994

John McCutcheon and Tom Chapin performed with the Winfield Regional Symphony for the first time.

1995

Aileen and Elkin Thomas performed with the Winfield Municipal Band on the band's one hundredth anniversary.

1996

The Avenue of Flags was started by Bob Flottman. In its first year, seven flags were flown.

John McCutcheon and Tom Chapin performed with the Winfield Regional Symphony at the premiere of McCutcheon's "Welcome the Traveler Home," which was written for WVF's twenty-fifth anniversary.

1998

A second attempt was made to make a world record largest guitar band (566 members).

1999

The IBMA recognized the Walnut Valley Festival as the "Bluegrass Event of the Year."

2002

The festival set a record attendance: 17,498.

2004

The National Finger Pick Guitar Championship became the International Finger Style Guitar Championship.

2014

Helen Avakian became the first female International Finger Style Champion.

2018

The arts and crafts fair was renamed in honor of Paulette Rush; its top honor was then called the Paulette Prize.

The First Feisty Music Camp for Kids was held.

The first Walnut Valley Farmers' Market was held at the campground.

2019

A record May rainfall flooded entire fairgrounds; City of Winfield employees cleaned and restored the fairgrounds in time for the Cowley County Fair and WVF 48.

2020

WVF 49 was postponed to 2021 because of COVID-19 pandemic.

The virtual WVF 48.5 took place as a fundraiser for artists and the festival.

2021

This was the first live Walnut Valley Festival since the beginning of the COVID-19 pandemic.

A beer and wine garden was introduced.

A livestream from Stage One was made available to all ticket holders.

2022

The Walnut Valley Festival celebrates its fiftieth anniversary.

Appendix B

ENTERTAINERS 1972–2021

Compiled by the WVA Staff
Edited by Orin Friesen

1972

Norman Blake
Bluegrass Country Boys
Country Gazette
Dan Crary
Jim and Jesse and the Virginia Boys
Lester Flatt and the Nashville Grass
New Grass Revival
Doc and Merle Watson

1973

Norman Blake
Bluegrass Country Boys
Dan Crary
J.D. Crowe and the New South
The Lewis Family
Sue Murphy
New Grass Revival
Red, White and Blue(Grass)
Doc and Merle Watson
Roland White

1974

Norman Blake
Bluegrass Association
Bluegrass Country Boys
Bluegrass Revue
Dan Crary
Jimmy Driftwood
Jimmy and Denzil Gyles
Ramona Jones and Friends
The Lewis Family
New Grass Revival
The Road Apples
Simmons Family
Tut Taylor
Doc and Merle Watson

1975

Cathy Barton
Norman and Nancy Blake
Bluegrass Association
Jack and Mike Theobald and Bluegrass Country
Bryan Bowers
City Limits Bluegrass Band
Dan Crary
Jimmy Driftwood
Rick George
The Gospelaires
Grand River Township
Don Lange
Dudley and Deanie Murphy
The Natural Grass
Reno, Harrell and the Tennessee Cutups
Larry Sparks and the Lonesome Ramblers
Tut Taylor
Happy Traum

1976, Walnut Valley Spring Thing

Byron Berline Band
Bryan Bowers
Country Cooking
Jimmy Driftwood
John Hartford
Hutchinson Brothers
Don Lange
Sue Murphy
New Grass Revival
Tut Taylor
Happy Traum
Merle Travis
Doc and Merle Watson and Frosty Morn
Pete Wernick

1976

Norman Blake
Byron Berline and Sundance
Bluegrass Attack
Roz Brown
Dan Crary
Rick George
Larry Hucke
Monroe Doctrine
The Natural Grass
New Lost City Ramblers
Red, White and Blue(Grass)
Butch Robins
Tut Taylor
Tecumseh
Thomas Singers (also known as Thomas Family)
Town and Country Review
Uptown Bluegrass Boys
Buck White and the Down Home Folks
Wooten Brothers

1977

Paul Adkins and Butch Mayer
Cathy Barton
Norman Blake
Jack and Mike Theobald and Bluegrass Country
Bryan Bowers
City Limits Bluegrass Band
Copeland Kids
Country Mile

Dudley and Deanie Murphy and County Line
Dan Crary
Jimmy Driftwood
Everybody and His Brother
Henry the Fiddler
Hickory Wind
Don Lange
Madeline MacNeil and Phil Mason
Richard Mason
New Grass Revival
New Lost City Ramblers
Uptown Bluegrass

1978

Cathy Barton
Norman and Nancy Blake
Bryan Bowers
Dudley and Deanie Murphy and County Line
Dan Crary
Malcolm Dalglish and Grey Larsen
East Creek
Cathy Fink and Duck Donald
Highwoods String Band
Don Lange
Madeline MacNeil and Phil Mason
McLain Family Band
New Cache Valley Drifters
Outdoor Plumbing Company
Harvey Prinz and Lilah Gillett
Red Rector and Bill Clifton
The Red Clay Ramblers
Mary Faith Rhoads and the Dobbs Brothers
Rosy's Bar and Grill
Sparky Rucker and John Davis
Art Thieme
Washboard Leo

1979, Walnut Valley June Jamboree

Ken Bloom
Guy Carawan
Bonnie Carol
Clanjamfrey
Cathy Fink and Duck Donald
George Gritzbach
Bruce Hutton
Joel Mabus
Magpie
New Cache Valley Drifters
Lisa Null and Bill Shute
The Red Clay Ramblers
Gamble Rogers
Sparky Rucker and John Davis
Ed Snodderly
Art Thieme
Jay Ungar and Lyn Hardy
Unity Bluegrass Band
Wrystraw

1979

Cathy Barton
Bluegrass Cardinals
Bryan Bowers
Country Ham
County Line
Dan Crary
Malcolm Dalglish and Grey Larsen
The Folk-Tellers
Front Porch String Band
David Holt
Hot Rize
Steve Kaufman
McLain Family Band
New Grass Revival

Peter Ostroushko
John Pearse
Harvey Prinz and Lilah Gillett
Mary Faith Rhoads and the Dobbs Brothers
Claudia Schmidt
Ed Snodderly
Talisman
Ed Trickett
Pop Wagner and Bob Bovee
Washboard Leo and His Mountain Men
Whetstone Run
Robin and Linda Williams

1980

David Amram
Cathy Barton
Norman and Nancy Blake
Booger Hole Revival
Bryan Bowers
Boys in the Band
Beverly Cotton
Dan Crary
Dulcimer Alliance
George Gritzbach
Frank Hill
Hot Rize
Just Bill (Hubert)
Front Porch String Band
Joel Mabus
Magpie
Mid-Missouri Hellband
Outpost Family Band
Harvey Prinz and Lilah Gillett
Kevin Roth
Claudia Schmidt
Art Thieme
Doc and Merle Watson
Wry Straw

1981

Backwoods Band
Cathy Barton and Dave Para
Berline, Crary and Hickman
Norman and Nancy Blake
Ken Bloom
Jack and Mike Theobald and Bluegrass Country
Bryan Bowers
Beverly Cotton
DeDannan
David Grisman Quartet
Neal Hellman
Hot Rize
Hotmud Family
Kimberlie
Front Porch String Band
New Prairie Ramblers
Jim Post and Randy Sabien
Harvey Prinz and Lilah Gillett
The Red Clay Ramblers
Mary Faith Rhoads and John Pearse
Denis LePage and Station Road
Art Thieme
Ron Wall
Washboard Leo and Nutra Frogs

1982

Cathy Barton and Dave Para
Becky Blackley
Ken Bloom
Bluegrass on Tap
Bryan Bowers
Company Comin'
Beverly Cotton
Country Gazette
Dan Crary
Mike Cross

DeDannan
Hoofin' High Country Cloggers
Hot Rize
Mark and Berit Kline
Dudley and Deanie Murphey
New Grass Revival
Paul and Win
Harvey Prinz and Lilah Gillett
Pumkin Center Revue
Red and Murphy and Co.
Mary Faith Rhoads and John Pearse
Kevin Roth
Southern Manor
Southwind
Orrin Starr and Gary Mehalik
Art Thieme
Undergrass Boys
Doc and Merle Watson

1983

Cathy Barton and Dave Para
Stevie Beck
Berline, Crary and Hickman
Ken Bloom
The Bluegrass Band
Roz Brown
Buck's Stove and Range Company
Dudley Murphy and County Line
Mike Cross
DeDannan
Tommy Flint
Foster Family String Band
Jim Fyhrie
Neal Hellman
Hoofin' High Country Cloggers
Maddie MacNeil and Seth Austen
John McCutcheon
Mark O'Connor
Harvey Prinz and Lilah Gillett
Chris Proctor
The Tony Rice Unit
Pat Skinner
Sleight of Hand
Southern Manor
Southwind
Art Thieme
Tisra-Til
Tracy's Family Band
Trapezoid
Washboard Leo
Whetstone Run

1984

Cathy Barton and Dave Para
Stevie Beck
Berline, Crary and Hickman
Becky Blackley
Bryan Bowers
Rolly Brown
Roz Brown
Danny Carnahan and Robin Petrie
Chameleon Puppet Theatre
Russell Cook
Patrick Couton and George Fischer
Foster Family String Band
Lindsay Haisley
Hot Rize
Juggernaut String Band
Joel Mabus
John McCutcheon
Larry McNeely Band
Walt Michael and Co.
New Grass Revival
Mark O'Connor
Southwind
Swiftkick Cloggers
Tennessee Gentlemen
Art Thieme

Touchstone
Trapezoid
Tony Trischka and Skyline

1985

Berline, Crary and Hickman
Becky Blackley
Blue Night Express
Roz Brown
Chameleon Puppet Theatre
Cloud Valley
Russell Cook
Mike Cross
Doug Dillard Band
Pat Donohue
Chris Duffy Trio
Green Grass Cloggers
Lindsay Haisley
Horse Sense
Hot Shandy
Pat Kirtley
Eric Lugosch
John McCutcheon
Nashville Bluegrass Band
Mark Nelson
New Grass Revival
Red Clay Ramblers
Mary Faith Rhoads and John Pearse
Gamble Rogers
Lynn and Liz Shaw
Art Thieme
Tony Trischka and Skyline
Washboard Leo

1986

Seth Austen
Cathy Barton and Dave Para
Stevie Beck
Berline, Crary and Hickman
Becky Blackley
Bryan Bowers
Roz Brown
Chameleon Puppet Theatre
Mike Cross
Dab Hand
Lindsay Haisley
Hoofin' High Country Cloggers
Hot Rize
Red Knuckles and the Trailblazers
Eileen Ivers
Maddie MacNeil
John McCutcheon
Mick Moloney, O'Connell and Keane
Mark O'Connor
Chris Proctor
Peter Rowan
Shady Grove Band
Special Consensus
Art Thieme
Aileen and Elkin Thomas
Ed Trickett
Tony Trischka and Skyline
Doc Watson and Jack Lawrence

1987

Linda Allen
Stevie Beck
Berline, Crary and Hickman
Becky Blackley
Roz Brown
Chameleon Puppet Theatre
Mike Cross
Foster Family String Band
Full Circle
Good Ol' Persons
Lindsay Haisley
Neal Hellman and Kim Robertson

Tim Henderson and the Belt Buckle Band
Hoofin' High Country Cloggers
Horse Sense
Hot Rize
Last Kansas Exit
John McCutcheon
Walt Michael and Co.
New Grass Revival
Red Knuckles and the Trailblazers
Harvey Reid
Hugh Sparks
Aileen and Elkin Thomas
Spontaneous Combustion
Total Strangers
Doc Watson and Jack Lawrence
Woods Tea Co.

1988

Cathy Barton and Dave Para
Bluestem
Roz Brown
Chameleon Puppet Theatre
Tom Chapin and Friends
Dan Crary
Mike Cross
Jim Fyhrie
Gary Gallier
Lila Gillett
John Hartford
Hoofin' High Country Cloggers
Hot Rize
Red Knuckles and the Trailblazers
Alison Krauss and Union Station
John McCutcheon
Walt Michael and Co.
No Strings Attached
Redwing
Reel World String Band
Harvey Reid
Mike Snider
Special Consensus
Carol Stober
Jack and Mike Theobald and Bluegrass Country
Aileen and Elkin Thomas
Turtle Creek
Doc Watson and Jack Lawrence

1989

Bell and Shore
Bennett Brothers
Berline, Crary and Hickman (and Moore)
Blue Rose
Bluestem
Bryan Bowers
Roz Brown
Buzzard Rock String Band
Chameleon Puppet Theatre
Tom Chapin and Friends
Danger in the Air
Cathy Fink and Marcy Marxer
Four Hands in a Cloud of Dust
Full Circle
Lilah Gillett
Steve Gillette
Anne Hills and Cindy Mangsen
Hoofin' High Country Cloggers
Laurie Lewis and Grant Street
John McCutcheon
Walt Michael and Co.
New Grass Revival
Harvey Reid
Phil Salazar Band
Shady Grove Band
Special Consensus
Spontaneous Combustion

Aileen and Elkin Thomas
Linda Tilton
Happy Traum
Turtle Creek

1990

Paul Adkins and the Borderline Band
Berline, Crary and Hickman (and Moore)
Bluestem
Roz Brown
Tom Chapin and Friends
Mike Cross
Danger in the Air
Julie Davis
Judy Dees
Dixie Chicks
Cathy Fink and Marcy Marxer
Four Hands in a Cloud of Dust
Gary Gallier Band
Lilah Gillett
Hamilton, Alewine and Fleming
Hoofin' High Country Cloggers
The House Band
Steve Kaufman
Andy May
John McCutcheon
Walt Michael and Co.
Northern Lights
Harvey Reid
Steve Smith
Special Consensus
Spontaneous Combustion
Art Thieme
Aileen and Elkin Thomas
Linda Tilton
Trapezoid
Happy Traum
Turtle Creek
Wild Rose Ensemble

1991

Cathy Barton and Dave Para
Stephen Bennett and Bill Gurley
Norman and Nancy Blake
Bluegrass Patriots
Bryan Bowers
Roz Brown
Dan Crary
Mike Cross
Danger in the Air
Julie Davis
DeDannan
Dixie Chicks
Mike Fenton
Lilah Gillett
Hoofin' High Country Cloggers
Steve Kaufman
Alison Krauss and Union Station
Loose Ties
Claire Lynch and the Front Porch String Band
Joel Mabus
Andy May
John McCutcheon
Lynn Morris Band
New Prairie Ramblers
The New Tradition
Mark O'Connor
David Schnaufer
Bill Sky Family
Spontaneous Combustion
Bill Staines
Aileen and Elkin Thomas
Linda Tilton

Happy Traum
Turtle Creek

1992

Paul Adkins and the Borderline Band
Stephen Bennett
Bluestem
Saul Brody
Roz Brown
Tom Chapin and Friends
Colcannon
Mike Cross
Dixie Chicks
Dennis Doyle
Friedlander and Hall
Front Range
Beppe Gambetta
Lilah Gillett
Steve Gillette and Cindy Mangsen
Jane Gillman
Slavik Hanzlik
Steve Kaufman
Laughing Matters
Andy May
John McCutcheon
Karen Mueller
The New Tradition
No Strings Attached
Andy Owens Project
Ranch Romance
Sparky and Rhonda Rucker and John Davis
Mary Caitlin Smith
Special Consensus
Spontaneous Combustion
Aileen and Elkin Thomas
Linda Tilton

1993

Cathy Barton and Dave Para
Bryan Bowers
Roz Brown
California
Julie Davis
Pat Donohue
Beppe Gambetta
Paul and Win Grace and Family
Steve Kaufman
Peter Keane
Alison Krauss and Union Station
Laughing Matters
Loose Ties
Andy May
John McCutcheon
Karen Mueller and Tom Schaefer
The New Tradition
No Strings Attached
Tim and Mollie O'Brien and the O'Boys
Andy Owens Project
Barry Patton
Tom Paxton
Ranch Romance
Revival
Scartaglen
Mary Caitlin Smith
Spontaneous Combustion
St. James's Gate
Ivan Stiles
Sugarbeat
Linda Tilton
Mark Tindle
Robin and Linda Williams
Radim Zenkl

1994

Duck Baker and Molly Andres
George Balderose
Bill Barwick
Stephen Bennett
Bluestem
Roz Brown
California
Tom Chapin and Friends
Cooper, Nelson and Goelz
Mike Cross
Julie Davis
Druha Trava
Cathy Fink and Marcy Marxer
Front Range
Crow Johnson
Makin' Memories
Marley's Ghost
Andy May
John McCutcheon
New Potatoes
The New Tradition
Nickel Creek
Nonesuch
Colm O'Maoileidigh
Barry Patton
Pfeiffer Brothers
Ranch Romance
Lou Reid, Terry Baucom and Carolina
Revival
Mary Caitlin Smith
Special Consensus
Spontaneous Combustion
St. James's Gate
Art Thieme
Aileen and Elkin Thomas
Linda Tilton
Winfield Regional Symphony
Radim Zenkl

1995

Bill Barwick
Bluegrass Etc.
Bluegrass Patriots
Bryan Bowers
Roz Brown
California
Tom Chapin and Friends
Mike Cross
Julie Davis
Phyllis Dunne
Friedlander and Hall Little Big Band
Beppe Gambetta
Steve Gillette and Cindy Mangsen
Crow Johnson
Steve Kaufman
Marley's Ghost
Andy May
John McCutcheon
Nickel Creek
Nonesuch
Tim and Mollie O'Brien and the O'Boys
David Parmley, Scott Vestal and Continental Divide
Barry Patton
Tom Paxton
The Plaid Family
Revival
Mike Seeger
Mary Caitlin Smith
Red Steagall and the Coleman County Cowboys
Aileen and Elkin Thomas
Linda Tilton

Winfield City Band
Young Acoustic Allstars

1996

Eddie Adcock Band
Charles David Alexander
Cathy Barton and Dave Para
Bill Barwick
Byron Berline Band
Blue Highway
Bluestem
Bryan Bowers
Roz Brown
Tom Chapin and Friends
Cherish the Ladies
Chesapeake
Dan Crary
Julie Davis
Pat Donohue
Beppe Gambetta
Grass Is Greener
Crow Johnson
Steve Kaufman
Steven King
Pat Kirtley
Marley's Ghost
Andy May
John McCutcheon
Karen Mueller Trio
The New Tradition
Nickel Creek
No Strings Attached
Tim and Molly O'Brien and the O'Boys
Mark O'Connor
Barry Patton
Tom Paxton
The Plaid Family
Revival
David Schnaufer
Mary Caitlin Smith
Spontaneous Combustion
Ivan Stiles
Aileen and Elkin Thomas
Linda Tilton
Winfield Regional Symphony

1997

Eddie Adcock Band
Cathy Barton and Dave Para
Bill Barwick
Stephen Bennett and Bill Gurley
Byron Berline Band
Black Rose
Bluestem
Roz Brown
Tom Chapin with Michael Mark and Jon Cobert
Cherish the Ladies
Dan Crary
Julie Davis
Judith Edelman Band
Freight Hoppers
Front Range
Beppe Gambetta
Dana Hamilton, Plus Two
Crow Johnson
Steve Kaufman
Loose Change
Marley's Ghost
Andy May
John McCutcheon
The New Tradition
Nickel Creek
No Strings Attached
Barry Patton

Tom Paxton
Chris Proctor
Bobby Read
Revival
Small Potatoes
Mary Caitlin Smith
Spontaneous Combustion
Aileen and Elkin Thomas
Linda Tilton
Ron Wall
Eric Weissberg

1998

Cathy Barton and Dave Para with Bob Dyer
Bill Barwick
Stephen Bennett
Bluestem
Bryan Bowers
Roz Brown
Tom Chapin with Michael Mark
Cherish the Ladies
Dan Crary
Mike Cross
Crucial Smith
Julie Davis
Bob Franke
Beppe Gambetta
Steve Gillette and Cindy Mangsen
Paul Goelz
Hickory Hill
Home Rangers
Leon Howell
Crow Johnson
Steve Kaufman
Laurie Lewis with Tom Rozum and Todd Phillips
Live Bait
Claire Lynch and the Front Porch String Band
Marley's Ghost
Andy May
John McCutcheon
Karen Mueller
The New Tradition
New West
No Strings Attached
Barry Patton
The Plaid Family
Small Potatoes
Spontaneous Combustion
Still on the Hill
Aileen and Elkin Thomas
Linda Tilton
Toucan Jam
Wild and Blue

1999

Carlo Aonzo
Bill Barwick
Stephen Bennett
Byron Berline Band
Blue Plate Special
Bluegrass Pals
Roz Brown
Crucial Smith
Pat Donohue
Connie Dover, Roger Landes and Friends
Euphoria Stringband
Nick Forster and Friends
Freight Hoppers
Beppe Gambetta
Adie Gray
Grubstake
Harmonious Wail

Crow Johnson
Steve Kaufman
Pat Kirtley
Dan Levenson
Marley's Ghost
Andy May with Jim Heffernan
John McCutcheon
Tim O'Brien and Darrell Scott
Pagosa Hot Strings
Barry Patton
Prickly Pair and the Cactus Chorale
The Renters
Ruby's Begonia
Safe Harbor
David Schnaufer and Stephen Seifert
Serenata
Small Potatoes
Special Consensus
Spontaneous Combustion
Ivan Stiles
Still on the Hill
Aileen and Elkin Thomas
Linda Tilton
Toucan Jam
Pete Wernick's Live Five/Plexigrass

2000

Bar D Wranglers
Cathy Barton and Dave Para
Bill Barwick
Stephen Bennett
Byron Berline Band
Big Twang
Bluestem
Bryan Bowers
Roz Brown
Michael Chapdelaine
Tom Chapin with Michael Mark
Cherish the Ladies
Crary and Hoppers and Their American Band
Mike Cross
Crucial Smith
Tommy Emmanuel
Beppe Gambetta
Los Harmonica Hombres y una Mujer
Home Rangers
Jana Jae and Friends
Crow Johnson
Steve Kaufman
Pat Kirtley
Kruger Brothers
Dan Levenson
Marley's Ghost
Andy May
John McCutcheon
Misty River
Karen Mueller
Nickel Creek
No Strings Attached
Barry Patton
The Plaid Family
Prickly Pair and the Cactus Chorale
Revival
David Schnaufer and Stephen Seifert
Small Potatoes
Spontaneous Combustion
Aileen and Elkin Thomas
Linda Tilton
The Wilders

2001

Cathy Barton and Dave Para
Bill Barwick
Stephen Bennett
Byron Berline Band
Big Twang

Bluestem
Roz Brown
Michael Chapdelaine
Tom Chapin with Michael Mark
Dan Crary
Julie Davis
Don Edwards
Exit 81
Fragment
Gallier Brothers
Beppe Gambetta and Carlo Aonzo
Hickory Project
Jim Hurst and Missy Raines
Pete Huttlinger
Kansas Heart
Pat Kirtley
Dan Levenson
Andy May
John McCutcheon
Misty River
Pagosa Hot Strings
Barry Patton
Prairie Rose Wranglers
Mark Schatz and Friends
Shenanigans
Small Potatoes
Sons of the San Joaquin
Spontaneous Combustion
Aileen and Elkin Thomas
Linda Tilton
Kelly and Diana Werts
The Wilders

2002

Bill Barwick
Stephen Bennett
Byron Berline Band
Bluestem
Roz Brown
Tom Chapin with Michael Mark and Jon Cobert
Mike Cross
Crucial Smith
Dakota Blonde
Julie Davis
Pat Donohue
Don Edwards
Tommy Emmanuel
Exit 81
Gallier Brothers
Beppe Gambetta and Carlo Aonzo
Henri's Notions
Hot Club of Cowtown
Jim Hurst and Missy Raines
Pete Huttlinger
Crow Johnson
Pat Kirtley
Laurie Lewis and Grant Street
David Mallett
Marley's Ghost
Andy May
John McCutcheon
Misty River
Karen Mueller and Robert Force
No Strings Attached
Barry Patton
Prairie Rose Wranglers
Red Wine
Sons of the San Joaquin
Spontaneous Combustion
Linda Tilton
Walnut Valley Men's Chorus
Kelly and Diana Werts
The Wilders
Brooks Williams
Yonder Mountain String Band

2003

Bill Barwick
Stephen Bennett
Roz Brown
Nick Charles
Classical Grass
Dan Crary
Julie Davis
Daybreak
Tommy Emmanuel
Pat Flynn, John Cowan and Friends with Stuart Duncan
Heartstrings
Hickory Project
Hot Club of Cowtown
Pete Huttlinger
Crow Johnson
Mark Johnson and Emory Lester
Marley's Ghost
Andy May
John McCutcheon
Modern Hicks
Karen Mueller
Kacey Musgraves
No Strings Attached
Barry Patton
Prairie Rose Wranglers
Prickly Pair and the Cactus Chorale
John Reischman and the Jaybirds
Small Potatoes
Special Consensus
Spontaneous Combustion
Linda Tilton
Walnut River String Band
Walnut Valley Men's Chorus
Barry Ward
The Wilders
Yonder Mountain String Band

2004

Cathy Barton and Dave Para
Bill Barwick
Stephen Bennett
Byron Berline Band
Bluestem
Roz Brown
Tom Chapin and Friends
The Chapin Sisters
Nick Charles
Cherish the Ladies
Dan Crary
Mike Cross
Julie Davis
Doyle Dykes
Tommy Emmanuel
Pat Flynn, John Cowan, Stuart Duncan and Scott Vestal
Gallier Brothers
Beppe Gambetta
Les Gustafson-Zook
Hot Club of Cowtown
Kane's River
Marley's Ghost
Andy May
John McCutcheon
Men of Steel: Dan Crary, Beppe Gambetta, Don Ross and Tony McManus
Barry Patton
John Reischman and the Jaybirds
Small Potatoes
Spontaneous Combustion
Alan Thornhill
Linda Tilton
Harry Tuft
Kendra Ward and Bob Bence
The Waybacks

Pete Wernick's Live Five/Flexigrass
The Wilders

2005

Bill Barwick
Stephen Bennett and Friends
Byron Berline Band
Roz Brown
Tom Chapin with Michael Mark
John Cowan Band
Julie Davis
Tommy Emmanuel
Steve Eulberg
Bob Evans
Pat Flynn and Friends
The Greencards
Adie Grey
Pete Huttlinger
Chris Jones and the Night Drivers
King Wilkie
Marley's Ghost
Andy May
Tim May and Plaidgrass
John McCutcheon
David Munnelly Band
No Strings Attached
Barry Patton
Sons of the San Joaquin
Spontaneous Combustion
Still on the Hill
Tennessee HeartStrings Band
Linda Tilton
The Waybacks
The Wilders
Williams and Clark Expedition

2006

Cathy Barton and Dave Para
Bill Barwick
Stephen Bennett
Byron Berline Band
Bluestem
Roz Brown
Cadillac Sky
Tom Chapin with Michael Mark
Nick Charles
Dan Crary and Thunderation
Julie Davis
Tommy Emmanuel
Pat Flynn, Buddy Greene and Friends
Bruce Graybill
The Greencards
Brian Henke
Hot Strings
Pete Huttlinger
Chris Jones and the Night Drivers
Steve Kaufman
Dan LaVoie
Marley's Ghost
Andy May
John McCutcheon
Andy McKee
Misty River
Mountain Smoke
David Munnelly Band
Tim O'Brien Trio
Barry Patton
Small Potatoes
Jo Ann Smith and Pocket Change
Spontaneous Combustion
Dave Stamey
Still on the Hill
Linda Tilton
The Waybacks

The Wilders
Adrienne Young and Little Sadie

2007

Bill Barwick
Bluestem
Ronnie Bowman and the Committee
Roz Brown
Cadillac Sky
Brad Davis, Tim May and John Moore
Julie Davis
Tommy Emmanuel
Pat Flynn
Beppe Gambetta
The Greencards
Greenwillis
Adie Grey and Dave MacKenzie
Michael Reno Harrell
Brian Henke
Pete Huttlinger
Kansas Heart
Marley's Ghost
Andy May
John McCutcheon
Mountain Smoke
David Munnelly Band
Alecia Nugent
The Old 78's
Barry Patton
Kenny and Amanda Smith
Dave Stamey
Still on the Hill
Linda Tilton
The Wilders
The Wiyos
Woods Tea Co.

2008

Bill Barwick
Stephen Bennett
Byron Berline Band
Roz Brown
Tom Chapin with Michael Mark
Dailey and Vincent
Julie Davis
Diamond W Wranglers
Beppe Gambetta
The Greencards
Buddy Greene, Ron Block and Jeff Taylor
Michael Reno Harrell
Brian Henke
Pete Huttlinger
Chris Jones and the Night Drivers
Randy Kohrs and the Lites
Marley's Ghost
Andy May
John McCutcheon
Adam Miller
Misty River
Mountain Heart
David Munnelly Band
The Old 78's
Barry Patton
Rockin' Acoustic Circus
Small Potatoes
Doug Smith
Kenny and Amanda Smith Band
Johnny Staats and Robert Shafer
Dave Stamey
Still on the Hill
Thomas/Delancey Trio
Linda Tilton
The Wiyos

2009

Bill Barwick
Stephen Bennett
Roz Brown
Tom Chapin with Michael Mark
Julie Davis
Beppe Gambetta
The Greencards
Buddy Greene, Ron Block and Jeff Taylor
Michael Reno Harrell
Brian Henke
Pete Huttlinger
Infamous Stringdusters
Wil Maring and Robert Bowlin
Marley's Ghost
Andy May
John McCutcheon
Adam Miller
David Moran, Joe Morgan and Friends
Mountain Heart
Mountain Smoke
David Munnelly Band
Notorious Folk
Barry Patton
Kati Penn and NewTown
Prickly Pair and the Cactus Chorale
Sawmill Road
Trevor Stewart
Still on the Hill
Linda Tilton
The Wilders
The Wiyos

2010

Bill Barwick
Roz Brown
The Chapmans
Nick Charles
Dan Crary
Julie Davis
Farewell Drifters
The Greencards
Hickory Project
Hillbenders
Houston Jones
Sierra Hull and Highway 111
Pat Kirtley
Randy Kohrs Band
Andy May
John McCutcheon
MilkDrive
Mountain Heart
Mountain Smoke
No Strings Attached
Notorious
Barry Patton
Prickly Pair and the Cactus Chorale
Kevin Roth
Small Potatoes
Trevor Stewart and Earthlines
Still on the Hill
Téada
Linda Tilton
Barry Ward
The Wilders
Josh Williams Band
The Wiyos

2011

Cathy Barton and Dave Para
Bill Barwick
Stephen Bennett
Byron Berline Band
Stephanie Bettman and Luke Halpin
Bluestem

Bryan Bowers
Roz Brown
Tom Chapin and Friends
Russell Cook
Dan Crary and Thunderation
Mike Cross
Julie Davis
Tommy Emmanuel
The Gallier Band
Beppe Gambetta
Hot Club of Cowtown
Pete Huttlinger
Eileen Ivers and Immigrant Soul
Pat Kirtley
Marley's Ghost
Andy May
John McCutcheon
Michael Martin Murphey, with
special guest Pat Flynn
Notorious
Barry Patton
Prairie Fire
Prairie Rose Rangers
Revival
Kenny and Amanda Smith Band
Trevor Stewart and Earthlines
Still on the Hill
Akihiro Tanaka
Linda Tilton
Mark Alan Wade Trio
Barry Ward
The Wilders
Josh Williams Band
The Wiyos

2012

3 Trails West
Bill Barwick
Stephen Bennett
Roz Brown
Dan Crary and Thunderation
Julie Davis
Driven
Steve Eulberg
The Greencards
Michael Reno Harrell Trio
Jim Hurst
Claire Lynch Band
Marley's Ghost
Andy May
John McCutcheon
Mountain Heart
NewFound Road
Notorious
Barry Patton
Prowell Family
Quebe Sisters Band
Revival
Jo Ann Smith and Friends
Richard Smith and Julie Adams
Steel Wheels
Still on the Hill
Téada, with special guest Séamus
Begley
Linda Tilton
Mark Alan Wade Trio
Barry Ward

2013

Bill Barwick
Stephen Bennett
Byron Berline Band
Roz Brown
Tom Chapin and Friends
Driven
Beppe Gambetta
The Grascals
Buddy Greene, Ron Block and
Sierra Hull
Haunted Windchimes

Pete Huttlinger
Marley's Ghost
Andy May
John McCutcheon
MilkDrive
Adam Miller
Mischievous Swing
David Munnelly Duo
Barry Patton
Prowell Family
Scenic Roots
Steve and Ruth Smith
Special Consensus
Dave Stamey
Steel Wheels
Still on the Hill
Tim and Myles Thompson
Linda Tilton
ToneBlazers
Winfield City Band

2014

Bill Barwick
Bettman and Halpin
Bluestem
The Boxcars
Roz Brown
Cherokee Maidens and Sycamore Swing
Detour
Driven
Fiddle Whamdiddle
The Greencards
Pete Huttlinger
Jacob Johnson
Kane's River
Andy May
Tim May and Steve Smith
John McCutcheon
Mischievous Swing
Joe Morgan and David Moran
Mountain Smoke
Barry Patton
Band of Ruhks
Revival
Allen Shadd, Jack Lawrence and T. Michael Coleman
Small Potatoes
Kenny and Amanda Smith
Socks in the Frying Pan
Dave Stamey
Steel Wheels
Still on the Hill
Tim and Myles Thompson
Linda Tilton

2015

Stephen Bennett
Byron Berline Band
Roz Brown
Tom Chapin and Friends
Cherokee Maidens and Sycamore Swing
Dan Crary, Bill Evans and Steve Spurgin
Della Mae
Detour
Driven
Green Flamingos
Michael Reno Harrell Trio
Pete Huttlinger with Mollie Weaver
Jacob Johnson
Marley's Ghost
Andy May
Tim May and Steve Smith
John McCutcheon

Notorious Folk
O'Connor Family Band
The Paperboys
Barry Patton
Prairie Rose Rangers
The Roys
Scenic Roots
Jo Ann Smith and Friends
Socks in the Frying Pan
Steel Wheels
Still on the Hill
Tannahill Weavers
Theory Expats
Tim and Myles Thompson
Linda Tilton
Barry Ward

2016

3 Trails West
Stephen Bennett
Byron Berline Band
Roz Brown
Ray Cardwell and Tennessee Moon, with special guest Pat Flynn
Chapin Sisters
Tom Chapin and Friends
Darin and Brooke Aldridge, with special guests Pat Flynn and John Cowan
Cherokee Maidens and Sycamore Swing
Crary, Evans and Spurgin with Martin Stevens
Detour
Driven
Juni Fisher
Pat Flynn
The Gallier Band
Beppe Gambetta
Green Flamingos
KBA Treblemakers
Brad and Ken Kolodner
Claire Lynch Band
Marley's Ghost
Andy May
John McCutcheon
Adam Miller
Mountain Heart
Tim O'Brien Trio
O'Connor Band featuring Mark O'Connor
The Paperboys
Barry Patton
Socks in the Frying Pan
Dave Stamey
Steel Wheels
Still on the Hill
Bryan Sutton Band
Tim and Myles Thompson
Linda Tilton
Barry Ward
Kelly Werts

2017

Stephen Bennett
Betse and Clarke with the Brushy Creek String Band
Roz Brown
Nick Charles
Della Mae
Juni Fisher
Bing Futch
GASS
Grass It Up
Chris Jones and the Night Drivers
Claire Lynch Band

Marley's Ghost
Andy May
Tim May and Steve Smith
John McCutcheon
John McEuen and Matt Cartsonis
Joshua Messick Trio
Adam Miller
The Outside Track
The Paperboys
Barry Patton
John Reischman and the Jaybirds
Mark Sganga
Socks in the Frying Pan
Steel Wheels
Still on the Hill
Linda Tilton
Wall-Eyed Moles

2018

Opal Agafia and the Sweet Nothings
Balsam Range
Stephen Bennett
Byron Berline Band
Roz Brown and Jim Ratts
Tom Chapin and Friends
Crary, Evans and Barnick
Bing Futch
Beppe Gambetta
GASS
Chris Jones and the Night Drivers
Marley's Ghost
Andy May
John McCutcheon
Joshua Messick Trio
Mountain Smoke
The Outside Track
Barry Patton
Mark Sganga
Jo Ann Smith
Socks in the Frying Pan
Dave Stamey
Steel Wheels
Still on the Hill
Billy Strings
Linda Tilton
Molly Tuttle
Barry Ward

2019

Muriel Anderson
Appalachian Road Show
Bryan Bowers Band
Roz Brown and Jim Ratts
The Cowboy Way
Della Mae
Bing Futch
GASS
R.W. Hampton
The Hootin' Annies
J2B2
JigJam
Chris Jones and the Night Drivers
Christie Lenée Trio
Ashley Lewis and Legacy
Matchsellers/Bluegrastronauts
Andy May
Tim May and Steve Smith
John McCutcheon
Old Salt Union
Barry Patton
The Quitters
Short Round String Band
Steve and Ruth Smith
Socks in the Frying Pan
Special Consensus
Still on the Hill

Linda Tilton
Kyle Tuttle Band

2020, Festival 48.5 (Virtual Festival)

3 Trails West
Appalachian Road Show
Helen Avakian and Dave Irwin
Stephen Bennett
Byron Berline Band
Roz Brown and Jim Ratts
Tom Chapin and Michael Mark
The Cowboy Way
Crary, Evans and Barnick
Damn Tall Buildings
Juni Fisher
Bing Futch
Beppe Gambetta
JigJam
Chris Jones and the Night Drivers
Marley's Ghost
Andy May
John McCutcheon
Mile Twelve
Adam Miller
Pretend Friend (Battle of the Bands winner)
Missy Raines
Mark Sganga
Socks in the Frying Pan
Frank Solivan and Dirty Kitchen
Steel Wheels
Steelwind
Mark Alan Wade and Kyle Baker

2021

3 Trails West
Appalachian Road Show
Rachel Baiman and George Jackson
Byron Berline Band and Legacy Grass
Roz Brown and Jim Ratts
Jo Ann Smith
Tom Chapin and Michael Mark
The Cowboy Way
Damn Tall Buildings
The Dillards
Bill Evans, Tim May and Steve Smith
Juni Fisher
Bing Futch
Beppe Gambetta
GASS
Gothard Sisters
Greystem
Ernie Hill
Chris Jones and the Night Drivers
John McCutcheon
Mile Twelve
Old Sound
Barry Patton
Pretend Friend
Missy Raines and Allegheny
Red Door Duo (Helen Avakian and Dave Irwin)
Mark Sganga
Allen Shadd and Kristen Holloway
Frank Solivan and Dirty Kitchen
Steel Wheels
Steelwind
Linda Tilton
Mark Alan Wade and Kyle Baker
Tray Wellington Band

ABOUT THE EDITOR

Seth Bate moved to Winfield, Kansas, in 1989 to earn a degree in music and theater from Southwestern College. He ended up falling in love with a Kansas farmgirl and a local music festival, and he stayed in the community. His interest in Kansas history was sparked by traveling Kansas for his work at the Wichita State University Community Engagement Institute and by teaching at the Kansas Leadership Center. Seth earned his master's degree from Wichita State's Local and Community History Program and holds a professional certified coach credential from the International Coaching Federation. Seth loves cooking, taking naps in a hammock and making his kids listen to loud '80s heavy metal. Follow him on Instagram: @sethinkansas.